Second time around

A practical guide to beginning life again

Second time around

A practical guide to beginning life again

Ron Ranson

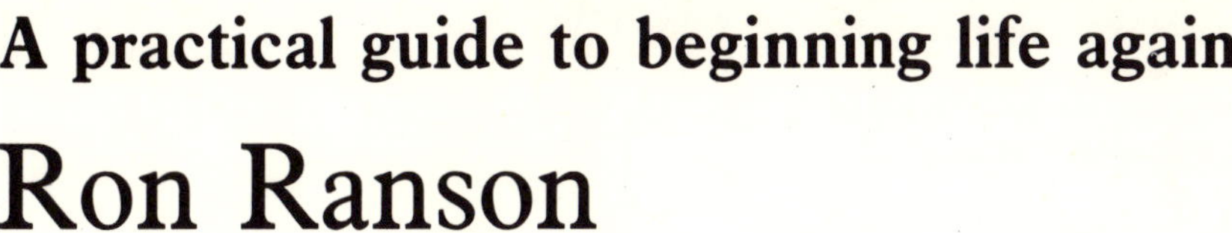

Illustrated by Graham Byfield

DAVID & CHARLES
Newton Abbot   London   North Pomfret (Vt)

British Library Cataloguing in Publication Data

Ranson, Ron
 Second time around: a practical guide to
 beginning life again.
 1. Success
 I. Title
 158'.1   BF637.S8

 ISBN 0-7153-8809-6

Typeset by Typesetters (Birmingham) Ltd
Smethwick West Midlands
and printed in Great Britain
by Butler & Tanner   Frome and London
for David & Charles Publishers plc
Brunel House   Newton Abbot   Devon

Published in the United States of America
by David & Charles Inc
North Pomfret   Vermont 05053   USA

Contents

Acknowledgements

I would like to offer my grateful thanks to my many friends and I *do* mean friends, most of them self-employed, who have helped me with this book.

Graham Byfield, working in Singapore, produced these beautiful, sensitive drawings entirely from my wild scribbles. Whilst I was determined to design the book myself from cover to cover, Karen Mitchell has helped me with hours and hours of collaboration in this direction, and her father, Ray Mitchell, took many of the photographs.

To my neighbour, Ann Mills, for her patient assistance with the manuscript itself. To my secretary, Liz Madge, who has typed all the copy and put up with my tantrums!

My thanks to *The Observer* for allowing me to use the chart on page 30 and to the Consumers Association for allowing me to use their weight chart on page 105.

Finally, I'm indebted to my patient and understanding wife, Audrey, who, as well as providing hundreds of cups of coffee at all hours, supported me loyally through this long task and even suggested the title for this book, *Second Time Around*.

Although not a great reader of poetry, the following quotation seems to sum up some of the spirit and purpose of this book, but I'm afraid I don't know where it comes from!

> Upon the wreckage of thy yesterday,
> Design the structure of tomorrow,
> Build strong corner-stones of purpose and prepare
> Great blocks of vision, cut from past despair.

Foreword

It could be said that I was one of Ron's 'victims'. Certainly since meeting him my life has every appearance of being a prize example of everything this book is about!

When I met Ron I was a senior manager and director in a large international company, beginning to 'burn out' and resenting the very little free time which I had to myself to devote to my hobby of painting.

Meeting and talking to Ron, who had done exactly what I dreamed of doing – turning a successful hobby into a successful business – made me realise that my dream was not impossible after all. Here was a man who had turned his back on the world of 'big business', and was deriving a great deal of enjoyment as well as earning a good living from what had been a pleasant hobby.

Many people in mid-career must ask themselves the same question, 'You only live once, so am I really doing the right thing?'

Clearly for some, the question has a much greater urgency than for others – for me it had become of paramount importance, but it took my meeting with Ron to give me the confidence to do something about it.

I now fell to some serious thinking and it seemed that I had to consider three alternatives – to continue in my present position, battling on, 'ducking and weaving', somehow surviving to what would hopefully be an early retirement. I could go back to an old success where there was still a space for me, or I could run my own show turning a hobby into a business. I decided on the last and suddenly my wife and I were out on our own as a painting and consulting partnership.

There was no large organisation to back us and to provide the regular income to deal with the all too regular bills. Many former contacts and colleagues were lost and (of great importance this) the only discipline is your own. We were starting again – I had to leave behind the sense of position and standing which went with the old career and strive to become firmly established in our new way of life.

We've made it now, my wife and I are much more fulfilled working as a team. My own job satisfaction has increased immensely as has our quality of life. However, I do feel that if Ron had written this book a few years earlier we could have avoided at least some of the pitfalls. At least we had his example – you have both! Make the best possible use of them!

Richard Everington
1986

Chapter 1
Having Fun

There comes a time in middle age when you should be able to relax and indulge yourselves a bit. You've done the best you can for the children while they were young, maybe struggled to get them through school and university – we went for six years without proper holidays to give our two boys a good education. But once they have 'flown the nest', it's time to take a good look at yourselves and plan your own future – just think – the chance to go out for a meal without multiplying the cost by four or five.

Great! But wait a minute – just as one part of you begins to see optimistic possibilities, often about this time along comes another thought – we'd better start saving for security in our old age while we can. This emotion is more likely if your self-confidence has been dented a bit along the way.

This need for financial security can easily become an obsession if you don't watch it. My own father was a dreadful warning to me. He was a loner most of his life, and left my mother when I was three years old. He was always very careful with his money, but he finished up wearing a top coat all the time in winter to save on heating bills and got very little pleasure out of life. There was absolutely no need for this caution as he died leaving several thousand pounds, carefully hoarded in various building societies.

This money came to me on his death and whilst I didn't blow it all on riotous living or world cruises, I did spend all of it on buying a piece of land that the whole family can enjoy and which is much more pleasurable than dull figures in an account book.

Being a different character altogether from my father, I enjoy spending

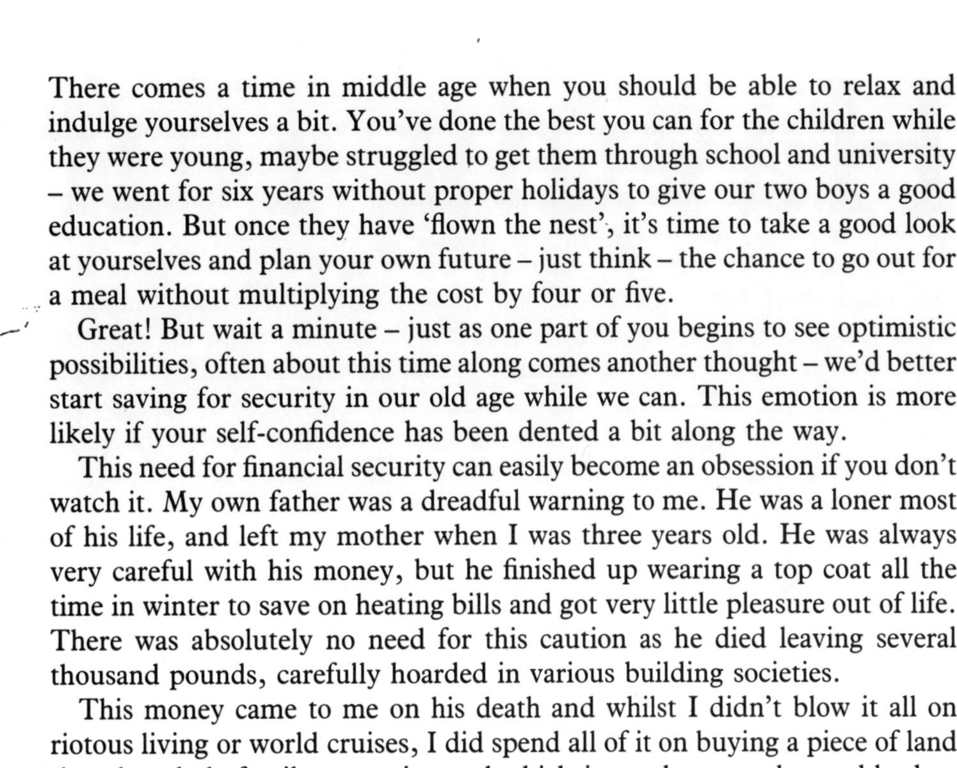

money, but my own temptation is to work too hard – not really for the money, but because I can't resist any new challenge – which doesn't leave much time for pure pleasure. We're constantly being told by our sons to go off and enjoy ourselves more. This may be the same problem in a different form.

Having bared my soul I now ask that you take stock of your own attitudes to life and search your own feelings and fears. It's a plea for you to put some joy in your life – perhaps to spend more money on yourselves – often quality of life can be raised by a quite modest expenditure, and after all, 'You can't take it with you'. Why not start by taking the opportunity, when your children leave home, to think about the house. Plan a completely different decorative scheme, perhaps creating a craft/study room, for you both to share, from what was once one of their bedrooms.

Redesigning the whole house to make the most of all living space can be like a tonic, especially if you and your partner both contribute ideas equally. Think about a new glazed extension to your living room – it may give a more intimate view of your garden. It's also too easy to put up with tired 1930s furniture just because it's been there for most of your life.

Let's look at a simple item like a mattress – we spend a third of our lives in bed, yet many of us put up with lumpy, sagging monstrosities years after they should have been chucked on the scrap-heap. Mattresses are only intended to have a limited life span, anyway, so get a new one. It will improve your back ache and it might even do wonders for your sex life too.

You should also look at your lighting – don't ever be mean with it, using a 60 watt bulb when you really need a 150 watt. Remember, your eyes need twice as much light at fifty years old than they did at twenty-five. Bad lighting, as opposed to subdued lighting, is very depressing too.

Clothes are another thing that we tend to economise on too much as we get older. I suppose we believe that at our time of life no one will bother to look at us anyway – this is utter rubbish. New clothes make a terrific difference, not only do they give you more self-confidence, but people do start looking at you in a new light. Even your children may comment with approval – especially if you ask their advice on 'dress sense'.

The next thing is to plan days out in order to visit interesting places, perhaps setting aside one day a week for a new adventure. Often the planning itself can be almost as satisfying as the trip. Even the theatre or a cinema visit with a meal afterwards can provide a highlight to your week, and all of us need some highlights to punctuate the routine of daily life. Mid-week break offers from country hotels are often wonderful bargains and there are also weekend break offers in London and other big cities where the shopping and a visit to the theatre make a lovely outing. Look in your local travel agent's window, then all you need is a little sense of adventure to make you try them.

Now let's talk about going further afield to other countries. Overseas travel not only provides new experiences, but it often seems to make one a more interesting person to know afterwards. Again, watch the local travel agent's windows for the last-minute offers of holidays in exotic places, often at unbelievable prices. These are obviously offered to fill empty seats on planes, but if you're now in a position to virtually drop everything at a few days' notice you can take full advantage of them. It's a good idea to really cultivate a reliable local travel agency and get to know them well.

There are all sorts of other ways of travelling on the 'cheap'. If possible always deal with an agent that offers Apex fares (Advanced Purchase Excursion), their fares can cut scheduled flights by as much as half. Another bargain is an ITX (Inclusive Tour Excursion), this is a cheap package tour ticket that includes a cheap fare with the holiday – sometimes it's even worthwhile using the ticket and throwing away the holiday. In any case, unless you're travelling in an emergency, never, ever, pay the full fare. For example, by studying the advertisements in the Sunday papers you can often save a terrific amount of money – shop around. Before travelling somewhere like Australia or South Africa I always get a few different quotes.

Some of the cheap package holidays especially in the 'off season' are so reasonable, it makes you wonder how they ever make a profit. You can often spend a month in Spain at an exclusive hotel in the middle of winter almost cheaper than you could live at home. But do watch for additions to the quoted price as these could add on another sixty per cent, such as for airport charges, single room supplements and fuel surcharges.

If you're visiting relatives in Australia or New Zealand, you can break your journey in all sorts of exotic places on the way, at little or no extra cost on a RTWT (Round the World Ticket). Being on a plane for twenty-five hours to Sydney is quite an ordeal – far better to have a few days in Hawaii where the temperatures remain in the seventies all the year round, or Hong Kong with its incredible vitality and drive, or Los Angeles where America is at its most blatant, full of achievers and escapists.

Now to motoring; if you decide to take your car abroad on the Continent, the secret is to make the ferry operators' rigid time tables work to your advantage – travelling at 2am rather than 11am you can often make big savings. Before you set off make sure that you hold a full British Driving Licence. An International Driving Permit is unnecessary unless you go to Eastern European Countries. By joining the EEC, UK insurance policies have been recognised as legal coverage by the other member countries. But remember this is only a legal minimum, so it's far better for you to take out a green card which provides the same cover as a domestic policy. If you're driving in Spain you should also take out a Bail Bond, which you can get from your insurer, because even a minor accident there can lead to the car being impounded and the driver imprisoned pending legal action. Watch your speed in Europe too, as most of the Continental police impose an on-the-spot fine. Also, don't forget the warning triangles, first-aid kits and spare light bulbs which are obligatory in many countries.

Here are a few tips which may prove helpful when travelling abroad. If you're flying it's a good idea to check luggage in early at the airport, as it seems that most of the lost luggage on certain flights was checked in late. Since airport theft is rife, the more valuable the contents of a case, the more battered and uninviting it should look. Another thing, it's advisable not to travel in your best clothes as you'll sleep much better and be more comfortable if you wear loose clothes, which can be rumpled without any regret. Free booze is another snare – often you'll arrive tired and listless, after even the briefest air journey, and blame it on 'jet-lag', but it's much more likely to be the effects of the alcohol and the altitude.

Here is some advice on money on holiday. Cash may seem the simplest method, but it is risky in large amounts. Small sums in sterling and the currency of the country you're visiting, however, could be useful. Traveller's cheques, which you get from the bank before you go, offer the best combination of security and flexibility. When buying the traveller's cheques you'll be asked to sign each one, and when cashing them at a bank or bureau de change – usually better rates of exchange than those offered at hotels or shops – you have to countersign in the presence of the cashier. Your passport is also needed as an additional form of identification. But banking hours abroad are often tricky so you should check on these locally when you arrive. It's advisable to take a small amount of local currency with you just in case.

When you're abroad don't keep all your money, whether it's traveller's cheques or cash, in the same place. Then even if you lose your wallet or handbag you won't find yourself penniless. If you intend to take foreign money with you, order it at least a week in advance from your bank. You should also remember that many countries restrict the amount of their currency you can take in or out, so make sure you check this with your bank first. And if you're taking traveller's cheques, keep a list of the serial numbers separately from the cheques themselves, and cross them off when you cash them, and then if your cheques are lost or stolen, you can claim a refund.

You'll get a full refund as long as the cheques were signed when purchased, and had not been countersigned. Report any losses immediately to the cheque company, or telephone them if there isn't a convenient branch to call at. You may have to wait until your return to the UK before you get a full refund, but you'll probably be provided with a certain amount of funds to tide you over. You can also use your credit cards to buy goods abroad. The main ones are Visa, Access and American Express, though I've found that American Express is the only one recognised all over the world. Access is accepted wherever you see the Eurocard or Mastercard symbols, and for Visa look for the blue, white and gold Visa symbol. Remember that you can always get cash with your cards if necessary.

Do have a go – I've found that most of my own globetrotting has been done since I reached fifty and hopefully there will be a lot more adventures to come in the future.

Chapter 2
The Crunch

This book is mainly aimed at five different types of people, all of you in your own way having arrived at the 'Crunch' – the decision time in your lives.

Perhaps you're already successful, you've achieved, more or less, what you set out to do in your chosen career, your talents have been recognised and you've been lucky enough to have one of the most important things in life – job satisfaction. In relative terms you've known the 'heights', but with retirement looming is it going to be downhill all the way from here?

Absolutely not! Self-employment is an ideal opportunity to retain the respect you've enjoyed over the years and keep your mind fully extended, and accept a new personal challenge. It's a chance to utilise all those other skills that previously have only been used in your hobbies, with, in your particular situation, probably the back up of a pension.

With my next character, the outlook is not so rosy. You may have a reasonably secure job with a monthly cheque coming in – but something is wrong. You've only been allowed to work on two cylinders, with your personality and ability only partly used. You may go home every night dissatisfied and frustrated by the management's attitude towards you. You may even have been passed over when the promotions came along. Now's the time to think seriously whether you should take a chance and go it alone, recover your dented self-respect and really show them what they've missed, before it's too late.

There must, also, be lots of you out there who've been thinking for months, or even years, of getting out of the 'rat-race'. You're probably under pressure in a stressful job, financially very rewarding, but is it worth the ulcers? Have you the courage to take a risk in exchange for peace of mind? Characters in these last two categories probably have the most difficult decisions of all to make and will really have to weigh up the options.

Sit down and take a cool look at your present situation and survey all the benefits you have at the moment and will have to forego. The main factor may be job security, but this will depend very much on your occupation. You won't be knocking off at five o'clock every day in self-employment. Nor will you get the perks of a company car, cheap travel or even a subsidised canteen. All these things will have to come out of your profits. You won't have the backing of a trade union, perhaps as a potential boss it may even become your adversary.

There's an enormous temptation to argue 'why risk all this for insecurity?' But, let's look at the advantages of self-employment. You get the freedom to work where you like and the incentive to expand and put into practice all your own ideas and to make your own decisions. Put down on paper a sort of 'profit and loss' account of what you stand to gain and lose by 'going it alone'. Then do a character analysis, which we're going to talk about later, and the answer should gradually be revealed.

The fourth type of person is, unfortunately, very common nowadays. You've probably always imagined that you had a good secure job until your retirement. Now you're suddenly faced with the cold fear of redundancy or even the more euphemistic 'early retirement'. It doesn't matter what they call it – you're too young to be on life's scrap-heap. The important thing to remember is that it's not *you* that's redundant, it's the job. When I got my cards from the personnel manager he said, 'You'll make it, Ron, you're young enough to start again'. I didn't believe him then, at fifty, but he was right. However difficult it may be at the time, convince yourself that this isn't the end, but a beginning of a new opportunity – one you may not have had the courage to take before. It's as if you were standing on the edge of a swimming pool, apprehensive of the shock of cold water. Then someone comes up behind you and pushes you – after the initial yells, you realise the water is really warm and wonderful. I would probably never have had the courage to give up my salary cheque voluntarily.

When you first lose your job you're likely to go through various stages of reaction. It can cause a sense of loss, much like a bereavement and in both cases your feelings will undergo various changes, until you reach the final acceptance. Knowledge of these emotions won't stop you experiencing them, but being forewarned might help. We're all conditioned into thinking our jobs provide us with a sense of identity, and when the job is lost we feel we've also lost our self-respect, as well as the respect of others.

Let's go through these emotions one by one. Probably the first will be numbness, almost disbelief that it could happen to you. It's like a bad dream from which you'll soon awaken. But much will depend on whether the news is sudden or if it's been a slow realisation of your future prospects. Amazingly, you may even have an initial feeling of optimism. After years of having to get up each morning and spend the day doing something you probably didn't like anyway, it may be an enormous relief when it comes to an end. If you do feel optimistic about the future, make the most of it – use it to carry you through all those necessary interviews with people with whom you may have financial dealings, such as the bank manager and building society. Start making plans now.

Another reaction is anger, particularly if you feel you've given your firm your best and that your predicament is really due to managerial incompetence. What you mustn't do is turn this anger or frustration inwards to yourself and your family. It's not your fault or theirs. You must, however, find an outlet for these feelings, so channel them into positive planning and action.

Inertia and lack of energy may be another emotion associated with job loss. You may feel increasingly lonely without the companionship of your colleagues and may even believe everyone's avoiding you, and it may be true; if you're depressed and afraid of losing face, you won't be very good company. But you must recognise these symptoms and fight them. Doing something positive is the best cure for depression and self pity. Try at least to see some humour in the situation and laugh about it with your family and friends – a lot of your pals will probably be in the same boat anyway.

The final emotion you have to recognise, and fight, is passive resignation – an apathetic acceptance of the situation. This is the time when you must really prove what you're made of. So start thinking positively, and plan your venture into a completely different way of life. Inevitably some of this stress will spill over into your marriage. If one of you loses your job, your partner may become apprehensive about the future too. A strained situation may develop if you're both at home all day and every day – perhaps for the first time since you started living together. The situation may worsen if you just sit around, not attempting to offer help in the house. In this new situation you may feel morally obliged to help, and imagine that by doing so you lose your dignity along with your job. It is at this stage that communication between couples is vital. It's a very difficult situation to adapt to, faced with a moody husband or wife, who is elated one day and depressed the next, especially when efforts of support may be spurned even though desperately needed. Unfortunately, there are problems on both sides in accepting this change in the relationship. To lose your job and identity at the same time is

indeed traumatic. We all have a need to be judged by our personal ability and by the kind of person we are. But the supportive partner's role may be equally difficult.

You may, however, be recently widowed or divorced and still coming to terms with the loss. Although grief and mourning are words nearly always associated with death, you feel grief and mourn a loss whether it's a spouse's death, a marriage ending in divorce or the loss of your job – they all have critical effects on lives. In each of these situations you have to adjust to the new circumstances by means of mourning, which is a way of coming to terms with loss. You must not, however, use grief as an excuse for attempting to retain other people's sympathy or for not making any effort to change your life. There comes a time when you must inevitably rejoin the mainstream of life. Don't be ashamed of your grief, it's a natural feeling and don't try to 'pull yourself together' too soon. The process must move at its own pace.

It may seem that a divorce is even harder to cope with than a death. When someone has gone forever you know that you must come to terms with it and start to build a new life. But a divorce may involve uncertainty and it may take a long time to realise that the marriage is really over before you can start to mourn it. Sadly, divorce is also associated with a sense of rejection and possibly feelings of guilt and failure. But there is a time in both these circumstances when, although you think that things have inevitably changed for the worst, you must try to rebuild your life constructively. It may even be possible to create an opportunity out of your loss. You may no longer have the support of a partner, but you can plan to strike out and prove you have the fortitude and flair to run your own small business. And if you still have children of school age to educate, it is a further incentive to play an active rather than a passive role, which you may have accepted hitherto.

As you have seen, there are many people from different circumstances who may want to start again by setting up their own small businesses. But lest I be accused of pushing you all, kicking and struggling, into self-employment, let me present you with some sobering thoughts, which may lose me half my candidates at this point.

It's certainly not going to be a 'soft option'. You'll probably have to work harder than you've ever had to before in order to get the business started. The work is always there, staring you in the face, reproaching you for not getting on with it instead of doing something else. It's more than likely that you'll have to work late into the evenings when you're tired out and would much rather be watching television with your feet up. The fact that no one is going to stand over you means that you'll need much more self-discipline and dedication. In many ways it's easier to go out to work, leaving all the undone household jobs behind – I still find it difficult to work with the distractions of home around. It's so easy to justify leaving money earning tasks to mow the lawn, especially on a warm summer day. Also you must realise that your standard of living may drop, possibly permanently, if things don't go right. You'll always have to make decisions, sometimes crucial to the business and sometimes unpleasant ones about sacking people – for this you'll need a certain amount of toughness. In any event, decisions must all be quantified

or you won't stay in business long. You'll have to exchange the support and companionship of your colleagues for a certain amount of isolation. It will be especially hard when facing moments of crisis and you'll need strength of character to pull you through some of these, in particular during the first year or two.

You must be reasonably healthy too, to stand up to the stresses of the business with its longer working hours, fewer rest days and perhaps fewer holidays – remember, there are no paid holidays in self-employment. Health should be of the utmost importance to all, not just the self-employed, and the section on Body Maintenance will be useful for everyone. Unfortunately, you'll probably have to give up many hobbies and outside interests if they get in the way of your business. I still miss my twelve years of amateur dramatics, but it became impossible to attend rehearsals regularly.

At this stage it's important to discuss all the possibilities with your family. Be absolutely honest with them and find out if they agree with your financial aims and ideas and are prepared, if necessary, to risk the family savings in the project. Their moral support, quite apart from actual help, will be vital, especially during the inevitable times of crisis and disappointment. Tell them candidly that you'll probably have less time for family life, and it may be a long time before the business is a financial success. Frankly, there's no standing still with a small business – it's either expanding or losing ground. If you don't work, there's no income. If the work you do isn't wanted and doesn't sell, the business will fail, and if it fails you'll get no redundancy.

I hope I haven't put too many of you off the idea completely as the time has come to take positive action and analyse yourself in an honest way. If you don't, you'll only be cheating yourself. You have to evaluate three things;

the sort of personality you have, what you have to offer and what your limitations are. You must size up your strengths and weaknesses – we all have weaknesses, but the important thing is to recognise and admit them. You can then choose a type of work that gives you the maximum opportunity for your strengths and the least possible call on your weaker points.

Are you an outgoing person, or a bit of a loner?

Are you a shy, sensitive person?

Are you cautious or decisive and thrusting?

Are your abilities intellectual or practical?

Are you authoritative or very tolerant and easy-going?

Are you methodical, with everything you do neatly set out, do you have a good memory for facts and figures?

Are you a conforming type or independent?

Are you eager for new challenges, ready to adapt quickly and accept possible improvements?

Are you 'people' orientated or production orientated?

Are you more respected for your technical expertise or do people look to you for a lead in situations?

Do you work best in dealing with lots of varied situations?

Do you enjoy playing with ideas and coming up with novel solutions?

Do you have a way with people that tends to keep their loyalty, and are you good at persuading and influencing them?

Do you have confidence in your own ability and does it come over when dealing with others?

Do you write and communicate well on paper?

Can you argue or negotiate persuasively and skilfully? Do you have a large vocabulary? Do people listen to you?

Do you prefer to tackle down-to-earth problems rather than speculate on theories?

Do you make pencil sketches whenever you can and think in three dimensions?

What skills have you previously used with your hobbies? These can have a considerable significance – they may highlight money earning talents hidden before.

What are your practical or creative skills?

Look frankly at some of the past successes and failures in your life and why they happened.

Could you be described as a 'workaholic' or a 'clock watcher'?

Try to think what other people have said about your previous work and what abilities they ascribed to you.

All these questions are vital as you're more likely to succeed if you're doing a job that matches as near as possible your profile of talents, skills, attitudes, interests and personality. It's a good idea to get an unbiased opinion from a good friend on your self-analysis. The section on 'Taking Action' will answer all these questions and also provide some positive suggestions. When I lost my job at fifty and was forced into taking stock of my life I had to answer a lot of questions but I'm thankful I carried on.

Chapter 3
My Own Story

Academically, I'm no great shakes . I was never actually bottom of the class at school, usually about an undistinguished twenty-fourth out of thirty. But there was one subject that I seemed to do better than the others, art. However, the careers master advised me that it wasn't a subject to earn a living from. I was therefore pushed into engineering, and became an apprentice with Rolls-Royce in my home town, Derby.

A couple of years were spent going from one workshop to another, learning my trade, until I was made technical writer on aero-engine handbooks. Some time after, a technical illustrator in the next department was sacked, he had spent so much time running his antique shop on the side that he was hardly ever there. I was round like a shot the next day to try for the vacancy and was given a cut-away fuel pump to draw over the weekend and was told, 'If it's any good, you can have the job.' I got it.

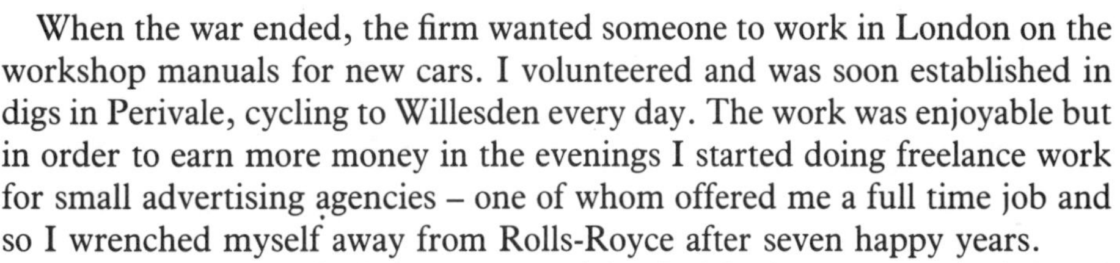

When the war ended, the firm wanted someone to work in London on the workshop manuals for new cars. I volunteered and was soon established in digs in Perivale, cycling to Willesden every day. The work was enjoyable but in order to earn more money in the evenings I started doing freelance work for small advertising agencies – one of whom offered me a full time job and so I wrenched myself away from Rolls-Royce after seven happy years.

During this time I had met a young girl called Audrey at a youth club and married her – she's still putting up with me after thirty-six years. After a while I moved to a larger advertising agency as a designer and crept into the advertising world through the back door, with no professional training at all – but I learnt the trade over the years. I worked for about half a dozen agencies during the next fourteen years, and at forty felt a bit 'long in the tooth' for all the high pressure. It was the right time for another change, so I applied for a job as a publicity manager with an engineering company in South Wales.

It was a quite dramatic change. My family had to be moved down to the countryside and by this time we had two boys of school age. After being one of the boys in the studio, suddenly my image had to change and I was behind a desk with my own secretary and staff. After being given a free hand I soon changed the company image with new colour schemes, new letterheads, brochures and advertising, as well as putting up exhibition stands in such places as Tehran, Moscow, Lagos and Copenhagen. Against everyone's advice and dire warnings we bought a big seven bedroomed house in the country with two acres of garden. This meant commuting sixty miles a day to work, which went on for ten years. It was too good to last for ever and eventually my boss left and the firm was taken over. The 'whizz kids' came in with their new ideas and although it had been a profitable company we had obviously been doing it all wrong before. The old gentlemen of the boardroom were eased out, industrial recession came along and the firm started to lose money. It became obvious that my days as publicity manager were numbered, and the 'dirty tricks' department decided to sack me for incompetence after twelve and a half years. They even did that badly and I was able to fight back so successfully that they offered to employ me as an outside consultant and paid me for two years afterwards – although I was never asked to consult.

Fortunately, this provided me with a breathing space and also gave me an idea – why not do the thing I did best for small firms who couldn't afford a full time publicity man? As a publicity consultant I went around to companies offering to spend a day a week with them, designing their literature, advertising and organising their exhibition stands, all for about £100 per month. It meant a lot of hard graft and travelling but I soon built up a clientele of five companies within a hundred mile radius. I then went to one or two printers and exhibition contractors and agreed a commission for all the work I brought to them. It all seemed to be dropping into place nicely. But after a few years of this work, I met a man in a pub who had organised an

Left: A painting of a wild garden in the Greek island of Paxos

Right: A painting of the Wye Valley in the mist

exhibition of local artists in a nearby castle. One of the artists had let him down, 'He promised a room full of paintings and hasn't come up with any,' he said. I must have been a bit sloshed at the time and said, 'I'll do you a room full.' He replied, 'Right – you're on! It's in a fortnight's time.' My art career had started. I bought some watercolours – they seemed less messy than oils and dried quicker. The paintings were very rough, but at least were finished on time and to my amazement a lot of them sold. I began to realise there might be some money in art after all. Next, came a week's painting course in Yorkshire, followed by a fortnight in the Pyrenees – I'd got the bit between my teeth now and couldn't stop. My methods and materials were unconventional to say the least, decorators' brushes instead of sables and meat trays for palettes, but my pictures were soon selling from the walls of local pubs.

At a painting weekend in a Teignmouth hotel, six months later, a fellow student asked me why I didn't start my own painting weekends. 'We'll all come,' he assured me, and so the Wye Valley Watercolour weekends began. My wife, Audrey, loved cooking, so while we painted she provided us with superb meals – everyone was happy and the weekends took off. We were forced to run more and more and now we run a course practically every fortnight. After about a year, my peculiar techniques were attracting attention and I decided to attempt an article in a painting magazine. The editor, with touching faith, gave me two to write. The magazine had a world-wide circulation and this began to bring people from as far away as Australia, Oman and South Africa to the house. By now the painting and teaching were taking over from the advertising consultancy, which was gradually phased out. One summer Audrey and I went off for a fortnight's holiday in Paxos, a tiny Greek island off Corfu. Whilst I was painting up in the hills one day along came two photographers, who were preparing literature for the travel firm that rented all the villas on the island. 'We want a picture of an artist for next year's brochure,' they said. It turned out that the company was planning to run painting holidays to fill the villas at each end of the season. On our return I immediately rushed round to the company's offices and offered to run their painting holidays and got the job. They flew me off each May and October for a fortnight in Paxos. They gave me a villa and paid me for each pupil taught – it was almost too good to be true. This went on for about five years and there were some incredible adventures, such as getting arrested for selling pictures without a permit, wading waist deep through floods and even having students marrying each other.

The following year some of my faithful band asked me to take them to Provence. These holidays began by my taking over a big, old farmhouse and filling it with painters for a fortnight. Painters as a crowd are an easy going lot, and by this time I was learning the psychology of running groups of people and maintaining their enthusiasm. One day I had a call from Winsor & Newton – they wanted me to be a demonstrator for them and visit art societies around the country. This fitted in nicely, as it meant I would be lecturing to the very people who were my potential customers for the weekends, and also get paid for it. I also went to another art material firm in Dorset, called Daler's, with some pictures under my arm, 'Could I be a demonstrator for you?' I asked. The company had never used one before, but just happened to be going to a trade fair in Milan the next month. 'Come with us and work on our stand.' It was hard work – eight hours a day for a week amongst hordes of excitable Italians. One visitor who owned a big gallery in Luxembourg pressed his card into my hand and suggested a one-man show there. I of course agreed. Daler's were pleased with the results and asked me to go to Chicago with them the following month, which also went well.

Meanwhile back at home a letter came from some of the Australians who had visited Wyeholme. They asked me to fly to Sydney to run some seminars and have a one man exhibition there. So I flew over for two weeks and it worked so well I went back again the following year. The Luxembourg exhibition was an absolute riot – I took sixty pictures over and after the British Ambassador opened the show the whole lot were promptly sold. There seemed to be plenty of money there, but no watercolours so the situation was ideal. I've just had my fourth annual exhibition there!

The next place I visited was South Africa, having received an invitation to demonstrate, lecture and have a one man show in Johannesburg. Whilst there I took the opportunity of touring round the country demonstrating to art societies. They made me feel so welcome, I repeated the trip last year but this time with different venues. By this time *Leisure Painter* had published about eight articles, and I took these along with my original paintings to a publisher and said, 'Could I write a book please?' In the end he agreed. I toiled for months – writing, painting and doing the lay outs – determined to do it all alone, in between my other activities if possible. The book eventually came out and took everyone by surprise, especially the publisher. It sold like hot cakes and was out of print in a month. It's now on its fourth edition within a year. Consequently, I now seem to be locked into another career as a writer, and this is my third book, with two more in the pipeline. This seemed to be a good time to cash in on the current video market so I got together with a production company to make an instructive film on watercolour painting. There had been a few done before, but they

were rather stilted and boring, and what we needed was something fast-moving and exciting. It's still on the market and selling very well all over the world and was seen recently by the Americans at the Frankfurt Book Fair. They decided it was better than anything already available in the States, so now they're launching it over there in a big way.

My life is full and rewarding. Getting the sack has proved to be the best thing that ever happened to me, though it seemed catastrophic at the time.

I hope it doesn't sound too easy – it wasn't. There have been plenty of downs as well as ups, especially in the early days of self-employment. It's important to grab *any* possible leads or opportunities that come along. Perhaps after reading this chapter you think that every lead taken up by me has blossomed – believe me it hasn't! Hundreds sank without trace, but at least I'll never have to say 'If only I'd followed that up'. On paper I'm a 'nothing' and haven't a single qualification. My painting, publicity, writing and acting abilities may not individually amount to much, but by squeezing every last drop of potential out of my limited talent and combining it with the practical knowhow picked up from previous jobs, I've managed to put together quite a formidable 'package'. Most of us have talents within us, often lying dormant until discovered later in life. But what you must do is to unearth all of those talents and make them work hard for you.

Now to get on with it. Let's first look at possible business action in detail. Incidentally, though I strongly believe that many people will be making a totally new start, many of the detailed points are actually as relevant to those who just want to take a new look at life and enhance their lifestyle at the time of retirement or to bring about a basic change in employment, marriage or whatever. This certainly goes for the chapters on health and sex that come at the end. The one other point is that while I advocate making a totally new start, there's everything to gain from good preparation. In particular, perhaps you've set your heart on being your own boss but have to stay in employment for the next year or two, try to make some preparations. It does obviously help to set a few hundred pounds aside and you can develop your ideas and build up contacts.

Chapter 4
Taking Action

This is the point where your experience, qualifications, ability, interests, personality and even weaknesses are all matched to one of the hundreds of possibilities open to you in self-employment. I'm not going to list them all here as there are other books which do this well and you'll find some useful titles in the last chapter.

Where do you start? Obviously if you have a specialised skill which is much in demand and which you thoroughly enjoy, your choice is easy – why try to run a hardware shop if you're a skilled osteopath, unless of course, you've become totally fed up with other people's backs. For the rest of you who have no obvious skills, the field can at least be divided into five different classifications. These are: manufacture, production, providing a service, creativity, and buying and selling.

Manufacture   If you want to do a skilled job which involves working with your hands and have lots of practical ideas and technical expertise, and are 'production orientated', manufacturing a product may suit you well.

This kind of business basically involves the use of equipment and raw materials to make consumer goods. You'll probably have to buy special premises and satisfy local zoning regulations for light or heavy industry. Unless you're working on products such as jewellery or leather work you can, normally, forget about working from home. Therefore, in most cases a certain amount of capital will be required to buy all the necessary equipment, stocks and premises. Obviously the product itself is the first consideration – the whole operation can stand or fall depending on its 'rightness'.

Do you really know what your customer wants? Perhaps it's something the customer is *not* getting at the moment. Try showing a prototype mock-up to your friends or customers, asking for comments, criticisms and possible suggestions. People are only too willing to help and the results will prove invaluable, whether the product is a screwdriver or a new type of rolling-pin!

It's most important to do your homework and find out all about your competitors' products. Study their advertisements, send for their literature and price lists and closely examine their products at trade exhibitions. Armed with this knowledge, you'll find how your potential product compares with others – has yours got any unique features? Why should customers buy yours rather than other products? Could any of their ideas be incorporated into your product without infringing copyright or patent?

Take a critical look at your product, try not to be swayed by tradition and what's been done before. Study the shape, size, quality, design and appearance – try to improve it. If the product is packaged, the pack design must be distinctive and tie up closely with your advertising. In many cases the customer won't see the actual product at the time of the sale, therefore the container will have to do the initial selling. It must also be strong enough to protect the product whilst in storage and during carriage. It is at this stage when you have an idea for a new product that you have to make a cool, clinical survey of the situation. Start by asking yourself some questions and write all the answers down.

What exactly have I got to offer?
Who will my customers be?
Where do I find them?
What competitors have I got?
In what way is my product better than theirs?
What's the best way of making my product known?

It's also vital to build up a profile of your prospective customers. Their ages, sex, social classes, temperaments, interests and where they work, live and play, even what sort of newspapers and magazines they read must be known. Then you'll be in a much better position to mould what you have to offer in such a way as to make it irresistible to them.

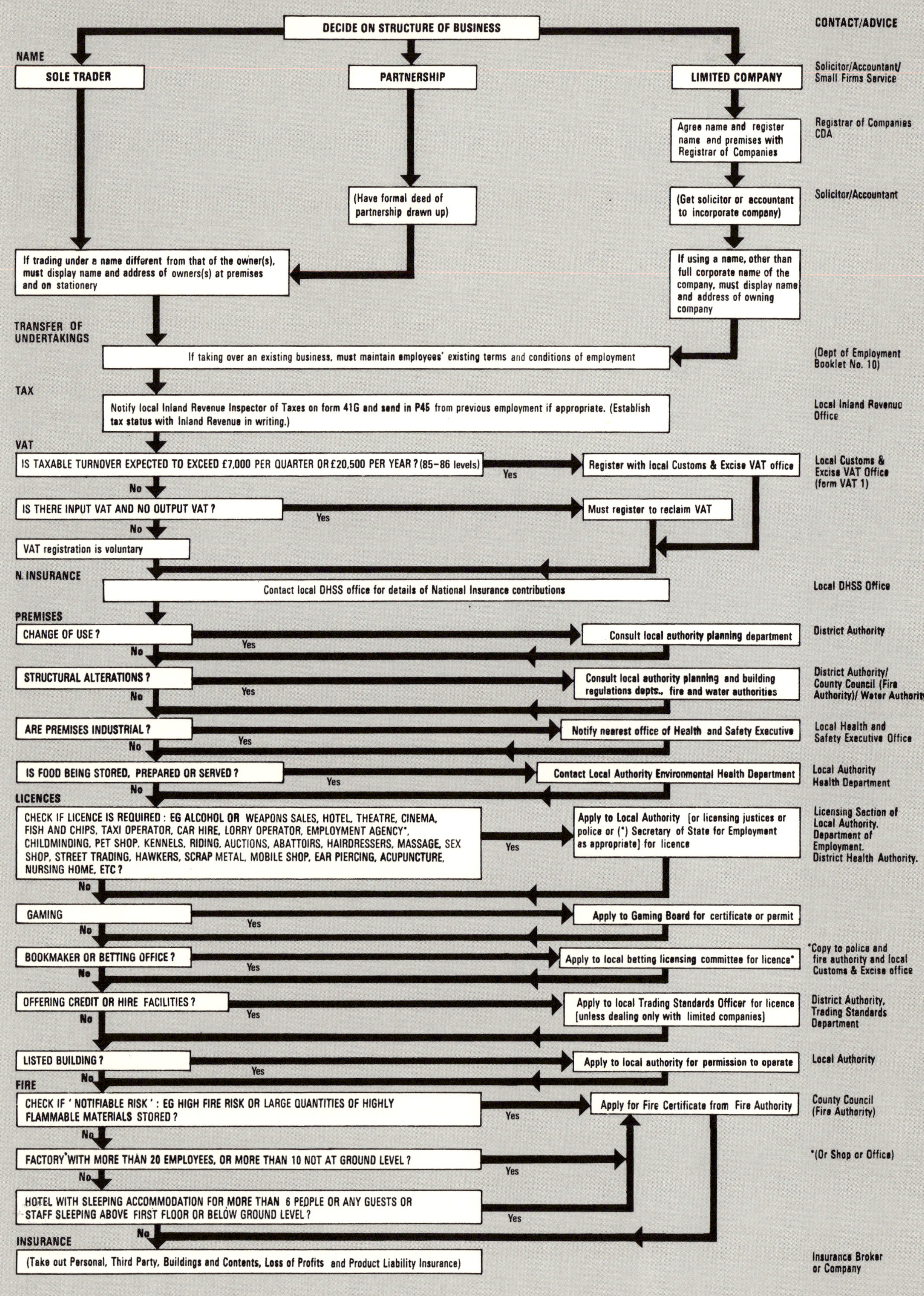

CONTACT/ADVICE
DECIDE ON STRUCTURE OF BUSINESS
NAME
SOLE TRADER
PARTNERSHIP
LIMITED COMPANY
Solicitor/Accountant/ Small Firms Service
Agree name and register name and premises with Registrar of Companies
Registrar of Companies CDA
(Have formal deed of partnership drawn up)
(Get solicitor or accountant to incorporate company)
Solicitor/Accountant
If trading under a name different from that of the owner(s), must display name and address of owners(s) at premises and on stationery
If using a name, other than full corporate name of the company, must display name and address of owning company
TRANSFER OF UNDERTAKINGS
If taking over an existing business, must maintain employees' existing terms and conditions of employment
(Dept of Employment Booklet No. 10)
TAX
Notify local Inland Revenue Inspector of Taxes on form 41G and send in P45 from previous employment if appropriate. (Establish tax status with Inland Revenue in writing.)
Local Inland Revenue Office
VAT
IS TAXABLE TURNOVER EXPECTED TO EXCEED £7,000 PER QUARTER OR £20,500 PER YEAR? (85–86 levels)
Yes
Register with local Customs & Excise VAT office
Local Customs & Excise VAT Office (form VAT 1)
No
IS THERE INPUT VAT AND NO OUTPUT VAT?
Yes
Must register to reclaim VAT
No
VAT registration is voluntary
N. INSURANCE
Contact local DHSS office for details of National Insurance contributions
Local DHSS Office
PREMISES
CHANGE OF USE?
Consult local authority planning department
District Authority
No
Yes
STRUCTURAL ALTERATIONS?
Consult local authority planning and building regulations depts., fire and water authorities
District Authority/ County Council (Fire Authority)/ Water Authority
No
Yes
ARE PREMISES INDUSTRIAL?
Notify nearest office of Health and Safety Executive
Local Health and Safety Executive Office
No
Yes
IS FOOD BEING STORED, PREPARED OR SERVED?
Contact Local Authority Environmental Health Department
Local Authority Health Department
No
Yes
LICENCES
CHECK IF LICENCE IS REQUIRED : EG ALCOHOL OR WEAPONS SALES, HOTEL, THEATRE, CINEMA, FISH AND CHIPS, TAXI OPERATOR, CAR HIRE, LORRY OPERATOR, EMPLOYMENT AGENCY*, CHILDMINDING, PET SHOP, KENNELS, RIDING, AUCTIONS, ABATTOIRS, HAIRDRESSERS, MASSAGE, SEX SHOP, STREET TRADING, HAWKERS, SCRAP METAL, MOBILE SHOP, EAR PIERCING, ACUPUNCTURE, NURSING HOME, ETC?
Apply to Local Authority [or licensing justices or police or (*) Secretary of State for Employment as appropriate] for licence
Licensing Section of Local Authority. Department of Employment. District Health Authority.
Yes
No
GAMING
Apply to Gaming Board for certificate or permit
No
Yes
BOOKMAKER OR BETTING OFFICE?
Apply to local betting licensing committee for licence*
*Copy to police and fire authority and local Customs & Excise office
No
Yes
OFFERING CREDIT OR HIRE FACILITIES?
Apply to local Trading Standards Officer for licence [unless dealing only with limited companies]
District Authority, Trading Standards Department
No
Yes
LISTED BUILDING?
Apply to local authority for permission to operate
Local Authority
No
Yes
FIRE
CHECK IF 'NOTIFIABLE RISK' : EG HIGH FIRE RISK OR LARGE QUANTITIES OF HIGHLY FLAMMABLE MATERIALS STORED?
Apply for Fire Certificate from Fire Authority
County Council (Fire Authority)
Yes
No
FACTORY*WITH MORE THAN 20 EMPLOYEES, OR MORE THAN 10 NOT AT GROUND LEVEL?
Yes
*(Or Shop or Office)
No
HOTEL WITH SLEEPING ACCOMMODATION FOR MORE THAN 6 PEOPLE OR ANY GUESTS OR STAFF SLEEPING ABOVE FIRST FLOOR OR BELOW GROUND LEVEL?
Yes
No
INSURANCE
(Take out Personal, Third Party, Buildings and Contents, Loss of Profits and Product Liability Insurance)
Insurance Broker or Company

Nothing has been lost on your product yet, if you decide after consideration that there's not a big enough potential market for you to make a profit, it costs too much to produce in its present form or there are already too many competitors offering the same product or it may be it's just not the right time to launch it. It's important to realise that the product will only succeed if you're making something that people need, at the time they need it and at a price that they're willing to pay.

Production   This area covers all those businesses involved with growing or breeding, from apple orchards and smallholdings to dog breeders and fish farms.

This kind of work will normally involve 'round the clock' availability throughout the year and may mean that in order to begin the job you will need to move house. You could write in a city flat but breeding pigs would hardly be suitable there. Previous experience is of prime importance in this area.

Providing a service   There are numerous opportunities for self-employment in this area and it's suitable for a business based at home.

The big advantage is that you're unlikely to need much, if any, special equipment and little or no stock, therefore, your initial demand for capital will be quite modest. Also, the equipment you do require shouldn't cause problems with storage or noise, so your neighbours shouldn't object! However, you will need previous professional experience for many of these projects. If, for example, you've had previous job experience as a hairdresser, electrolysist or beautician, you could get clients to come to your home – but you'll probably need planning permission first (see page 84). And if you're an experienced book-keeper, or typist, you can advertise your services locally and charge by the hour, these skills are usually in great demand.

In many projects you may have gained previous knowledge and experience from a hobby, but it's important to get further training, such as at evening classes, to reach a higher degree of skill. Remember, you'll be competing against established professionals so you'll have to approach your new venture in a similar manner. There are usually a great variety of courses, evening class, day-release, correspondence, residential or even full-time. Your local college will be able to advise you on courses offered, such as clock repairing, upholstery, china repairing and restoration and many more. When it comes to services like dressmaking, people expect a higher standard than can be obtained from ready-to-wear clothes. You could study for a City & Guilds Certificate, before charging for your services. Even if you decide to use your skills as a cook, to provide meals in your home, sell your cakes, pies and jam or prepare dishes at home for other people's parties, lunches or receptions, it is advisable to perfect your skill at a technical college or adult institute first. Don't forget either the various regulations you'll need to

Opposite: 'Flow Chart' to show various procedures necessary when starting a business

comply with if you intend to provide food for the general public. But persevere; around the world several groups of women have brought new interest into their lives and money into their homes by serving breakfasts in other people's houses.

You may use your expertise as a past employee to start a consultancy or agency. Define your scope as closely as possible and relate it to your own expertise, dealing with areas and products which you know best. To illustrate this point, my elder son, who trained as a barrister, recently decided that he wanted to leave his job with a pharmaceutical company and become self-employed. The initial idea was to form a team of lawyers, accountants and marketing men to provide a complete service to small businesses. After sending out questionnaires and receiving various business reactions over six months, it gradually became obvious that the whole operation would prove to be too complex and risky. He realised that what he should do was set up as a consultant in pharmaceutical law – the subject he knows best and where he had virtually no competition. He has now started his own business, persuading his previous employer to become his first client. It all seemed obvious with hindsight but the first idea created the initial excitement and impulsion to bring about the eventual changeover. In all these projects, it's still important to do your market research beforehand – find a need for a service locally and fill it, be it bicycle repairing, contract gardening or picture framing.

Creativity If you enjoy working with materials or tools in a creative and inventive way and have an artistic or craft skill to offer, and also experience gained from an existing hobby, this could be the right avenue for you to explore.

This is an ideal opportunity to fulfil the growing demand for craftsman-made 'one-off' objects that the big companies can't supply. This covers many areas, such as cabinet making, picture and antique restoring, and wrought iron work. If you enjoy working with words, ideas and feelings, it may be that you could earn your living as a writer or freelance journalist. It's like any other trade, you've got to think of your customer first. In this case, it's the editor or publishers and you must make sure the product fits their needs completely. Which is the best way to go about it? Start by doing your marketing properly. Before you even begin to write get hold of a copy of the *Writers' & Artists' Year Book*, and go through it thoroughly. It has all the information on magazines, newspapers, publishers, literary agents, advice on copyright, typing services and even how to correct proofs.

Next, go to a good book shop and spend several hours studying the competition objectively. Then find a publisher who specialises in your chosen subject. Non-fiction publishers seem to specialise in various areas. One I know, deals mainly in art, railways and military matters. When writing non-fiction, write about the subject you know best and put it over in a direct and conversational style. It must be readable and convey as much information as possible in a concise and interesting way. It sounds common sense, but there

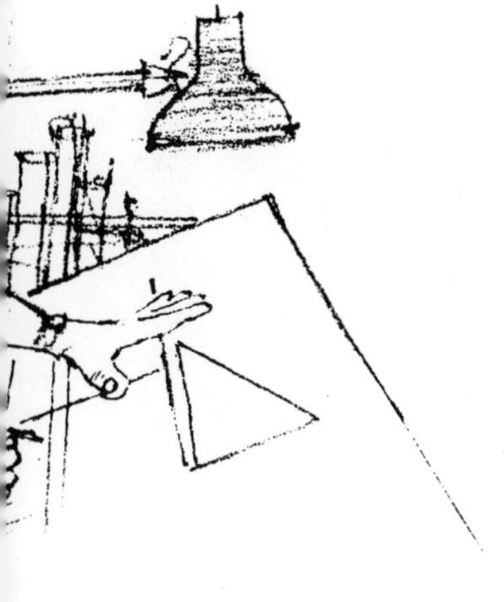

are lots of boring books around. It's the 'honing down' process that really makes the difference. Fiction is of course divided into various categories, such as romance, westerns, thrillers, historical and science fiction – and you'll have to resign yourself to fit into one of these slots. It may be advisable to learn your trade by writing magazine articles before leaping straight into writing a book. It can teach you a lot, especially about economy of words. It also brings other benefits such as providing you with good examples of your writing style which may be invaluable in persuading the publishers of your first book that your book could be a good seller.

For those interested in painting, there seems to be an intense desire in these days of mass production to own an original painting. Unfortunately, there's an enormous communication gap between artists and the public. The public hears of enormous prices paid for works by famous artists, and even sees works of art by unknown artists make hundreds of pounds and is put off. The trouble is that most artists are bad at marketing and perhaps at communication outside their craft. Writing from personal experience it is possible to make a good living out of painting – without special training, if the pictures are sold properly and at a reasonable price to the right market.

Buying and selling The quality needed here to succeed is an ability to persuade and influence others; you should be 'people orientated'. If you're too shy and withdrawn, you probably won't sell well.

In this category of business you will probably need special premises, such as a shop or a warehouse, where the goods can be stocked, displayed and sold. The secret of success is a high turnover, which means plenty of stock, bought on short-term credit, which it is hoped will be sold before it needs to be paid for. But a small shop can also be a home as well as a business, though this could be risky if the shop fails, as you might lose your home too.

As always, it's very important to know your business well beforehand. Take antiques, for example; it's easy to be drawn towards this because you may have always had an interest. In this case your stock is not brought to you weekly by a wholesaler, you'll have to be a 'hunter', haggling at sales rooms with other dealers, in street markets or fêtes to buy stock. The same thing applies to running a book shop; it's not enough to love books and the people who buy them. It would be useful to work in a second-hand bookshop first for a while, to gain experience on how to obtain stock, and most important how to make a profit at it. Whether your shop prospers or not depends on several factors. The site must be chosen carefully – not too near a competitor, but readily accessible to the public. Ideally there should be car parking facilities nearby, double yellow lines everywhere will keep customers away.

Research into an area before setting up a business is important. For instance, if a local factory closes down, you might lose half your customers, and it would be foolish to open a grocery business without finding out first whether a supermarket is about to be built close by – unless of course you planned to sell delicatessen items not available at the supermarket. As soon as your shop opens, you must project your own personality into the business, giving it a definite character and building a good reputation and customer loyalty.

If you eventually decide that you don't want to risk 'all' in a new venture, you could always buy a small established business. There are agents who specialise in retail businesses such as pubs, restaurants, small hotels or sub-post offices. These obviously demand capital, but you dramatically reduce your chances of failure and at least you do get a roof over your head, which means there's a lot more capital to spare. Seventy per cent of people buying small businesses are doing it for the first time. Their capital is probably derived from a redundancy payment or a lump sum from a pension, together with the sale of their house. You would probably need a minimum of about £25,000, but with about £40,000 you could expect to buy a substantial business. If you are interested in a sub-post office, for example, the range is quite large and at any one time there may be at least 120 offices available to choose from. You can hardly go wrong with a sub-post office, because you're provided with a regular income in the form of a post office salary. You also have the potential for further developing the retail side of the business as it's an ideal opportunity to sell your range of goods, be it hardware, jumpers or pottery, to all the people who walk in through your door. Also in a rural sub-post office, you may be the only shop for miles.

Buying a pub on retirement is a fantasy many people have – beware. A pub is a great deal of hard work, it's not just laughing with the customers. If your only experience has been on the drinking side of the bar, you probably won't last very long. It would be much better if you thought about a tenancy before taking on a freehold.

Another way of starting your own business, without too much risk, is franchising. This is a half way stage between being employed and self-employed. It works on the basis that in return for a sum of money, you're allowed to trade under a nationally recognised name, you own your establishment but you use the products, expertise, know-how and reputation of a big company. Franchise businesses are to be seen everywhere, for example, Wimpy Bar, Golden Egg, BMS driving schools, prontaprint, Kentucky Fried Chicken, Dyno-Rod, Spar groceries, Little Chef, to name but a few. This kind of arrangement has many advantages – you get the exclusive right to sell in your area and gain from their national advertising and brand images, as well as benefitting from the expertise and practical experience of others. The disadvantages are that you're committed to buying goods from the company and paying royalties to it and having set opening-hours. The company also dictates the design of your shop and the uniforms to be worn. The average cost of a franchise is about £30,000 – quite an investment, but few such businesses fail. Your contract lasts from seven to ten years, so make sure you get legal advice first. The rewards can be high, but be prepared to work long and hard hours especially in the early years. However, do take care as there are quite a few 'cowboy' franchisers about. It would be sensible before you sign any contract, to visit other franchisees under the same banner, and find out if they're satisfied with the parent company. You can also get further advice from the British Franchise Association; you'll find the address at the back of this book.

Whichever business you decide to go in to, there are three different ways of structuring it. All three have their advantages and disadvantages, but in the end it's entirely up to you to weigh them up and decide which is the best method for you. Your alternatives are to work as a sole trader, a partnership, or a limited liability company.

As a sole trader, 'one-man' business, you're regarded as a private individual and as such are entirely responsible for your business. However it doesn't necessarily mean that you have to work alone and you may employ staff to help you. You will be able to trade under your own name or under a registered business name and you are entitled to take all the profits of the business, but if things go wrong you are held responsible. If you can't pay your debts, your creditors can take all your personal possessions in settlement, these could include not only your home and car, but even your clothes and furniture. This all sounds a bit pessimistic but you must be warned. This arrangement is probably best for businesses providing a service, such as a writer, artist or window cleaner, as you won't have to take too many financial investment risks. I'm a sole trader as it suits my own particular circumstances ideally and it's always possible to change to another legal identity if advised by an accountant. One more warning, if a sole trader dies the business effectively ceases and any employees can then claim redundancy money, which would have to come out of the estate. In order to pay the debts the family of the deceased may have to sell the house to pay up, so it's sensible to protect against this contingency with life insurance.

A partnership is set up when between two and twenty people get together to trade as one firm, sharing the profits between them. A partnership is quite easy to set up, but you should only do it after very careful thought. It's rather like a marriage, so don't do it just for the sake of having company.

Your prospective partner or partners must really contribute some specialist expertise to complement your own skills otherwise you're just giving away part of a potentially valuable asset. You must also be absolutely sure that any future partners are completely trustworthy, as each partner is legally responsible for the debts of the others, including their tax bills. If a partner decamps, leaving unpaid bills, the other partner or partners will have to stump up to pay them. As in the case of the sole trader your creditors can take all your possessions. If you decide to set up a partnership, make sure you do it with the help of a solicitor. The agreement should state each person's share of the profits, the value of his share if he wants to get out, also what would happen if one partner died, or a new one came in. Some professional partnerships, like dentists or vets, may be just an agreement to share the services of receptionists and typists, with each partner drawing his own fees independently.

Due to all the risks involved in being a sole trader or being part of a partnership, many people decide to set up as a limited company, and they become a limited liability company. The big advantage is that by trading as a company your personal liability is protected by law, and shareholders can only lose the money that they've actually invested in the company. In return for this concession a limited company must put 'Limited' or 'Ltd.' after its name to warn people who might be lending it money or providing goods. But being a limited company doesn't mean that the banks will immediately queue up to lend you money. On the contrary, they may ask the directors for personal guarantees that the loan will be repaid despite the limited liability. There are other advantages though, it can cut your tax bill if you pay higher rates of income tax and can provide you with the chance of a good pension more cheaply. However, if you set up a company you'll no longer be regarded as self-employed. As a director of the company you'll be treated as an employee, liable to pay tax under PAYE and Class 1 National Insurance contributions. Your own accountant or solicitor, given all your circumstances, will be able to tell you whether forming a company could be worthwhile in your case. He'll then help you set the whole thing up, as it's a fairly complicated procedure. Certain legal documents must be drawn up, and you must have a registered office and register with the Registrar of Companies. It may cost you about £150 to do all this.

A limited company is obliged to send the complete accounts each year to the Registrar of Companies, so that anyone can look through them if they're intending to do business with the company. Therefore you must take into consideration the cost of having the books audited, together with other formalities and fees each year.

Each person in the group involved in setting up the business should contribute something to the company; either cash, expertise, equipment or goodwill, in return for a share in the company's profits. They then become shareholders and directors. If someone wants to get out of the business his share in the company can be sold to the other shareholders, or even to someone outside. If a shareholder dies, the share can be passed on to heirs or sold.

The quickest and usually cheapest way to set up a limited company is to buy a ready made one 'off the shelf'. This can be done by going to a company registration agent, who is listed in the *Yellow Pages*. The agent will probably give you a whole list of companies with fictitious names and the agents' staff will be listed as directors. You'll need to supply new names and a new address for the register and when you've paid the fee the agent does the rest. Once the company is established you can then change the name at any time to suit the real company. This method may all sound a bit dodgy, but I can assure you it's a perfectly legitimate way of starting a limited company.

Never be afraid of taking advice, the best way of gaining knowledge is to talk your ideas over with other people. Two heads are better than one and often the more heads you use the better. Speak to friends and relatives and bounce your ideas off them. You'll be surprised how rewarding this can be.

Ask people to be absolutely frank, even brutal, and if any criticism of your project recurs it's advisable to rethink it because you're probably talking to potential customers. Also, speak to other people in your own trade or profession and test their reactions, but don't tell them *all* your ideas. You'll need to balance their advice against the fact that they may eventually become direct competitors.

Try not to be blinkered and become besotted with the first idea and insist on persevering with it, no matter what. It may be that the product will only sell if it's completely redesigned, aimed at a different section of the market or made in a different material. It may be you'll have to admit that it's simply a non-starter. It's far better to call off a wedding the week before than be divorced a year later.

Chapter 5

Do's and Don'ts for Success

There are obviously reasons why some people succeed in business and others don't, and I would like to be perfectly honest in this chapter and lay bare all my ideas, thoughts and prejudices. Some of them you may violently disagree with, but I hope at least to provoke you into some constructive thinking – lets call it 'business philosophy'. We shall also look at the things which spell the difference between success and failure in any enterprise.

At one time we seemed to be the workshop of the world. Our cars were better made and more reliable than any others, and so were our planes, ships and motorcycles. What went wrong? Why were we overtaken and left standing in so many things? As well as all the usual excuses, I believe the real reason is that we were outpaced by the other countries with a combination of energy, drive and better marketing skills. We just stood around shrugging our shoulders and complaining that we couldn't possibly compete.

In my last job as a publicity manager I travelled to trade fairs all over the world and had the opportunity to compare our engineering products and sales methods with those of other countries in the same market-place. My company gradually lost its lead over its foreign competitors, not because the product wasn't as good, but it was the usual story of sales letters not being

answered for weeks, and broken promises over deliveries, while our competitors were prepared to work all night getting quotes which would then be delivered by hand and placed on the prospective client's desk next morning. We had a unique product, originally streets ahead of its foreign competitors but we sat back on our laurels while others took our basic idea and improved upon its design and marketed it in a much more aggressive way. It's hardly surprising that the customers, faced with a similar product

and a cast-iron delivery date and efficient service, succumbed even though originally they might have preferred to buy British. A prime example is the motorcycle industry which was supreme a few years ago. The Nortons, the Velocettes and the BSAs were household names, then along to the Isle-of-Man races came the Japanese with little note-books. By diligent work and consumer research they found out what improvements the customer would like to see, such things as pressbutton starting rather than kick-starting. The final result, as everyone knows, was the wholesale collapse of the British motorcycle industry over the last few years and a virtual monopoly by the Japanese.

The British were not the only ones to be taken by surprise and outflanked industrially. The German camera industry's Leica and Rolleiflex were legends in their field until a few years ago, but one hardly sees them now.

The Swiss watch industry can teach us all a vital lesson. Up until twenty years ago, it had an unrivalled reputation and controlled the world market in watches. The trouble was that the managements were too conservative and cared little for innovation and marketing. They relied smugly on their past reputation and regarded the Japanese as shoddy imitators, and Hong Kong with contempt. The consequences were disastrous. They hung on to the top end of the market with Omega and Rolex, but the middle of the market was savaged and they virtually disappeared from the bottom end. From exporting eighty million watches in 1970, they dropped to eighteen million in 1983 out of a total world market of 400 million – the rest was completely dominated by Japan and Hong Kong. Their biggest mistake was to ignore the microchip until it was too late. Their failure to convert, early enough, from mechanical to electronic movements cost them dear, more than two thirds of Swiss watch firms have disappeared in the last twenty years. But along came Dr Ernst Thomke, who was marketing manager and later managing director of the Swiss subsidiary of Beechams, the pharmaceutical giant. He was asked to join the watch manufacturer for whom he had worked briefly as a lad. He knew little about watches but he did understand marketing. He decided to leave the middle of the market to the Japanese, and went for the lower end. He produced a cheap but revolutionary moulded case which had the moving parts mounted directly on to it. He forgot about fancy designer names and called it 'Swatch'. It was a sensation and quickly became an international cult item, produced in bright colours including tartan and lace patterns. In some watches perfume was injected into the straps. Crazy perhaps, but it worked, with sales now reaching eight million a year. Dr Thomke is now concentrating on revitalising the top end of the market too, so that he can squeeze the Japanese from both ends. Meanwhile the Far East is paying him the ultimate compliment – they're busy trying to copy him. The important thing is to learn from past mistakes and at all times be positive and constructive. Let's learn from the Japanese and beat them at their own game as Dr Thomke did so successfully. All we need basically is more energy and drive and marketing skill than they have, preferably on a national scale.

When it comes to original ideas we are supreme. Half the world's

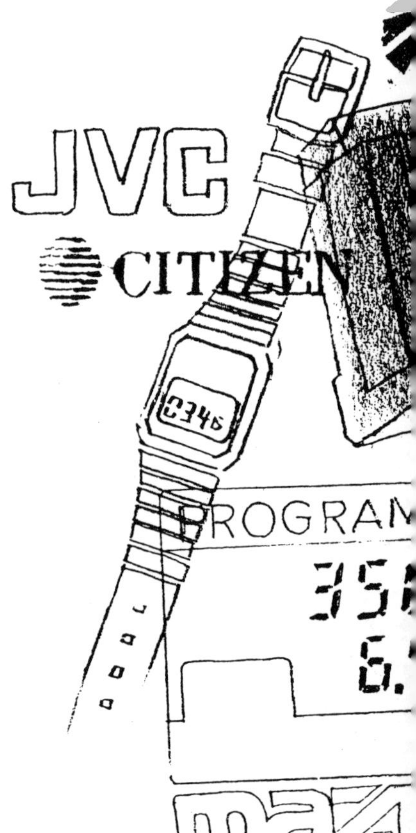

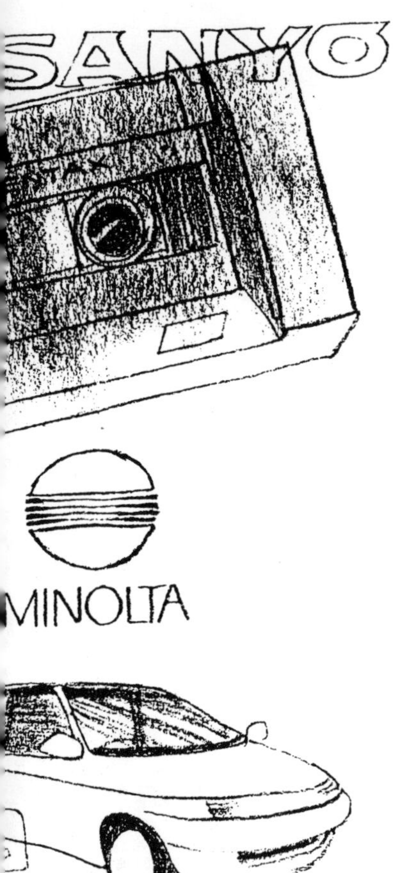

inventions seem to have come originally from Britain, but we don't seem to be good at exploiting them fully. Frustrated inventors have to go abroad with cap in hand to get their ideas financed and as a result the foreigners grow fat on our brains. As a prospective or embryonic self-employed person you have a wonderful opportunity to cut yourself away from the frustrations of large companies. You no longer need to rage at the inadequacies of the sales or marketing departments. You're both now, and the managing director – and the tea-lady as well, for that matter. Once you've become accustomed to the challenge of going it alone you'll have complete freedom to work on your own initiative without having to please your boss, or suffer the inevitable internal politics. The change that has come over me since I've been on my own has been enormous, my mind seems to be working at twice the speed it did before. I also believe that in being self-employed, common sense is far more valuable than academic degrees and that the most important attributes for success in self-employment are indeed *energy, drive* and *marketing skill.*

I'm often asked, 'Where do you get all your energy from?' when doing my exhibitions, art courses, books, lectures, videos and business trips abroad. 'You've got more than a normal bloke half your age!' But I'm afraid I can't remember being particularly energetic as an employee. I did work hard from 9am–5pm, but probably like many other people started looking at my watch at about 4.45pm. On my own I'm carried along by this wave of excitement

and the thought of the limitless possibilities of tomorrow, next week or next year. As you've already seen, every single opportunity or lead is jumped on and followed up. Always go after twice as many opportunities than you can possibly handle, half of them will probably go down the drain anyway. Being self-employed is like being an animal in the wild, walking through the forest, ears and eyes alert for the slightest sound and sight, always ready to pursue its quarry as opposed to being an animal in captivity, feeding with all the others at the communal trough – I know which *I* prefer.

Another important thing is to give value for money. Try to pull out all the stops and give your customers more than they expect. It's a very rare thing nowadays and will probably get rarer. So many firms and businesses want to give you the bare minimum as soon as they have hold of your money. With regard to my own field it has been known for some art instructors to disappear for hours in the middle of a course, to do their own paintings perhaps, while the disgruntled pupils are left on their own. Having suffered this in the past I spend every moment with my pupils (I suspect some of them wish I'd go away at times) but I've built up a good reputation for this and there are more prospective pupils than I can possibly handle.

The person who does my picture framing, doesn't hand over the finished product to his customers as most do, but every one is delivered in a pristine plastic bag. His prices are incredibly competitive too. As a result his firm has grown from a two-man business to the biggest framers in Wales within just a few years. Word of real value-for-money spreads like wildfire, and is worth any amount of advertising. Your best salesman is always a satisfied customer. About eighty per cent of my own business has been built up by word of mouth and only about twenty per cent by advertising. Build constantly on your success and use it as a key to open the next door. If you're making bespoke furniture for example, photograph your best works and build up an album to impress future clients and as a result obtain even more work. This was the case when I started my writing career, I took published articles to a publisher and persuaded him to publish my book. It's a mistake to stand still when you have enough work for the time being or believe that you're well enough known not to bother with advertising. Keep publicising yourself even when you're rushed off your feet. Smiths, the crisp maker, is a good example of standing still. At one time it was virtually the only firm in the field, and was probably a bit complaisant, especially with its advertising. Then suddenly the company was surrounded by highly publicised competitors such as Golden Wonder and many more. I advertise every month in my particular magazine even when I'm booked up for nine months ahead. You can't beat consistency, otherwise people may think you've gone out of business or have died.

Reliability is of the utmost importance too; it was broken promises that cost my last employers. Always commit yourself to a definite delivery date and keep to it no matter what happens, even if you have to work all night, the night before. It should be a matter of pride and honour to you as nothing makes you lose credibility so fast as failure and lame excuses. It's also quite common to put off starting a job for any number of reasons and then trying to justify it by filling your time with minor jobs – the official name for this is 'lateral displacement'. Although it may seem like a small point, try to reply to letters and enquiries promptly – it does make an impression. Many's the time I've had a booking letter which started 'Thank you for your prompt reply'.

As a self-employed person, friendliness, openness, cheerfulness and willingness can be very profitable virtues. Your manner can attract customers or keep them away, and your telephone technique is also important, even if you're turning them down because you've got no more room or you're out of stock! You should make maximum use of your own unique attribute, your personality. Wherever one goes it seems that businesses often stand or fall on the strength of their owners' personality – a pokey little backstreet pub can be constantly swarming with customers due mainly to the landlord's warm and welcoming personality. Conversely, a miserable or disagreeable landlord can empty a pub within a month.

A pushy, domineering salesperson can make customers afraid to go into the shop, whereas a clever one makes a friend of the customers, notes their sizes and tastes and quietly suggests things that might appeal to them. To my great delight I've found an outfitter like that, as a result he makes a lot of money out of me, and I really admire his technique. The personalities of travel couriers and schoolteachers make an enormous difference to their charges – they can make or mar a holiday, or make a subject fascinating or dry as dust.

As for employing other people, is it any wonder that so many self-employed people vow they won't employ anyone outside their own family circles due to all the fuss about rights of employees and trade unions, even if

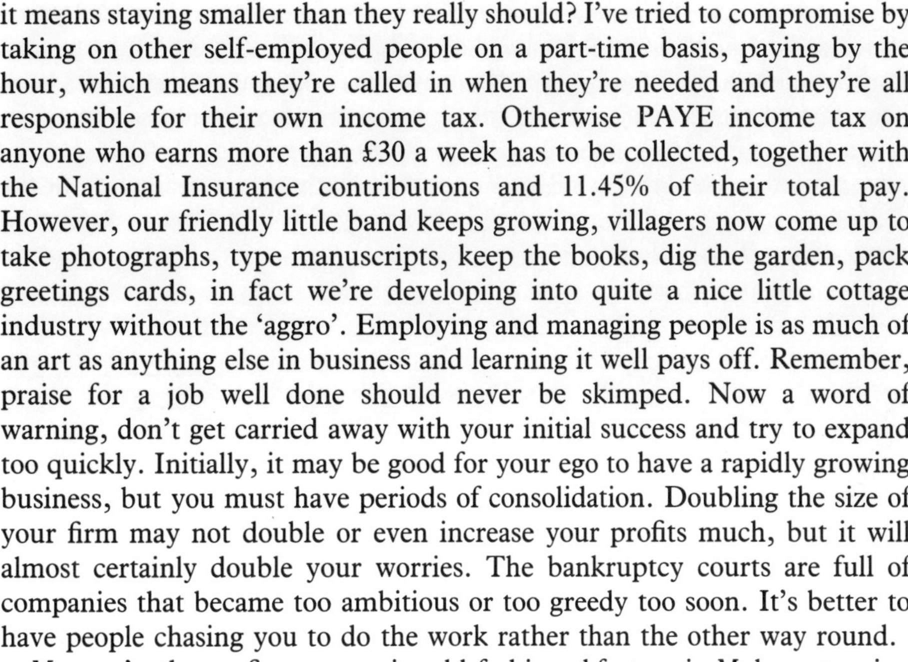

it means staying smaller than they really should? I've tried to compromise by taking on other self-employed people on a part-time basis, paying by the hour, which means they're called in when they're needed and they're all responsible for their own income tax. Otherwise PAYE income tax on anyone who earns more than £30 a week has to be collected, together with the National Insurance contributions and 11.45% of their total pay. However, our friendly little band keeps growing, villagers now come up to take photographs, type manuscripts, keep the books, dig the garden, pack greetings cards, in fact we're developing into quite a nice little cottage industry without the 'aggro'. Employing and managing people is as much of an art as anything else in business and learning it well pays off. Remember, praise for a job well done should never be skimped. Now a word of warning, don't get carried away with your initial success and try to expand too quickly. Initially, it may be good for your ego to have a rapidly growing business, but you must have periods of consolidation. Doubling the size of your firm may not double or even increase your profits much, but it will almost certainly double your worries. The bankruptcy courts are full of companies that became too ambitious or too greedy too soon. It's better to have people chasing you to do the work rather than the other way round.

Morgan's, the car firm, are a nice old-fashioned factory in Malvern turning out vintage sports cars in the traditional manner and with a very happy workforce, most of whom have been with them all their working lives. They have about a five year waiting list for their cars and an almost fanatical, loyal clientele. The secondhand value of the cars is often higher than the new ones because of the scarcity. Everyone is happy and secure so why on earth should they expand wildly and try to compete with the big boys? With a nine month waiting list for courses it's tempting to take on an assistant and even more students, but I've built up my business on my own individual personality and it would be so easy for things to become impersonal, and a lot of goodwill and probably a lot of money would be lost in the process. Instead, my solution is to take on more part-time secretarial and other help in order to release me to do all the things I do best, such as teaching, writing and painting, and they do all the things that I do badly.

It's essential to keep fully abreast of modern developments that may help you as a one man business. As you reach middle age you may be apprehensive of modern electronic equipment and avoid it. The buttons seem to get smaller and multiply, while the lettering on them becomes even more difficult to fathom, but if you take courage and try to master it, it can make your working life so much more efficient, and it can even be fun when mastered. Over the last year or so my business has slowly expanded and I've taken on, and learned to control reasonably well, a calculator (I still don't trust it yet and do every calculation twice just to check); an electronic typewriter which is one stage further ahead than an electric one; a hand-held, battery driven dictaphone which is carried around in the pocket, and is like an electronic notebook with tiny tape cassettes that hold about half an hour's talk. The tape is then slipped into my secretary's machine which is worked by a foot pedal. This was the method used when writing this book.

I also have a cordless 'phone. It has a range of about two hundred yards which spares me that awful business of sprinting from the top of the garden to arrive just as the ringing stops. I always wonder what opportunities have been missed when that happens. It also has a memory facility so that I can dial a list of pre-set numbers just by pressing one button. If you decide to have one, make sure that it's BATB approved (with a green seal on it), or the Telecom engineer will whip it out indignantly the first time he comes to service the official 'phone.

Photo-copying machines seem to be constantly leap-frogging over each other with new developments. It's advisable to lease rather than buy one initially as it can then be changed periodically when the next improvement comes along. The photocopier in use in my office is my third. It can réduce and enlarge at the touch of a button and more uses are constantly found for it. Answer phones are useful in a business, especially if a lot of your time is spent away from the office. Much as I dislike them, my next purchase will probably be an answer phone, but rather than the usual stilted message you hear and which puts you off completely, I shall probably say 'Look, I hate these things as much as you do but give me your number and I'll ring you back.' It would be very useful if once a month you stop thinking about your day-to-day problems and consider exactly what you're really trying to achieve, and what you've achieved so far, and what you'll need in order to reach your next goal. You'll have a much better chance of getting there if you know your destination beforehand. To sum up briefly what's already been said, you can practically guarantee success by pinpointing your potential clients, finding out exactly what are their specific needs and going to enormous trouble to see that they get it, on time and at a competitive price — it's called common sense.

Lastly, don't be put off by the pessimism of others, especially in areas where there is not much of a tradition of self-employment and enterprise. In New York every taxi driver seems to be earning extra money with a definite objective in mind, bettering himself, educating the children, or whatever. Too many Britons say it can't be done. It can!

Chapter 6

How to Promote Yourself

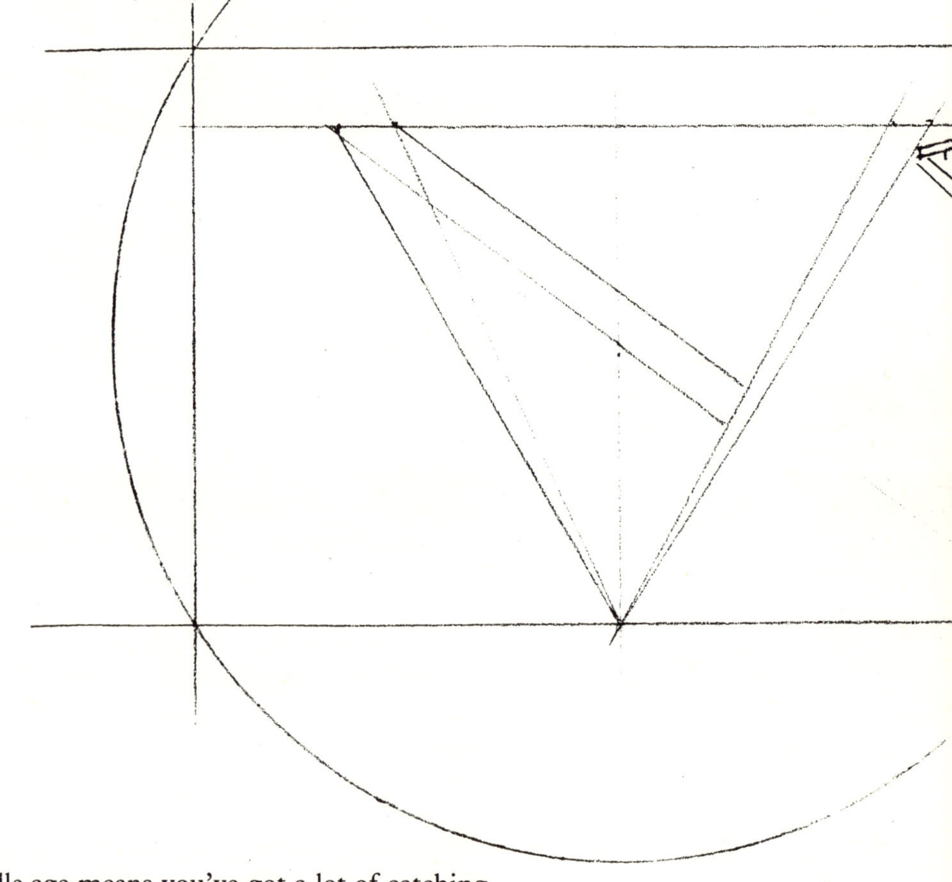

Starting up a new business in middle age means you've got a lot of catching up to do, quickly. You have to short circuit the gradual 'build-up' process and try to make sure that you arrive virtually overnight. This may sound impossible, but it *can* be done with energetic and consistent promotion, often in the form of advertising and public relations (PR).

Word of mouth is one of your best and cheapest ways of building up your business and your greatest salesman is a satisfied customer, but promotion is an essential part of your overall plan. It can range from a modest postcard in a newsagent's window or an entry in *Yellow Pages*, right through to a personal television appearance. It covers stationery, literature, advertising, lecturing and public relations, but don't shy away in terror – just read how simple it can all be. It was fortunate that before starting up my own business

I had been with various London advertising agencies for fifteen years, and later a publicity manager in a company for twelve years. During that time I dealt with everything, from beer to children's shoes, and from knitwear to industrial valves. But the basic principle involved in all these commodities was the same, so it was easy to bring all this past experience to bear when selling one product – myself. By using every trick in the book, it has cost very little in terms of money but the results have been very satisfying. In this chapter I want to pass on as many tips as possible – many of the ideas being basic common sense and homespun psychology anyway. You'll easily see how you can apply them to your own circumstances.

The first step, and a very important one, is to choose an appropriate title for your proposed business, it's the one thing that people will remember you by in the future. What may spring to mind first is to put your own name to it, but it could also be a description of your particular product or service. Probably the best way is to make a long list of possible names, also using suggestions from friends, and from this list one name will usually stand out as being the best. For instance, when my younger son started his own business he first thought of calling it Ranson Marketing, but it became obvious that it would be much better to use his christian name instead, which was shorter and sounded more thrusting, so it became Lance Marketing. If you do use a title other than your own name without any addition, you'll have to register with the Register of Business Names. You'll find the addresses at the back of this book. You can't, of course, register any name you like. They won't normally let you use words like, royal, queen, king, princess or crown for example, or they may feel that you're implying that the business is bigger than it really is if you try to call yourself Global Enterprises and you happen to be a local window cleaner. I even had a bit of a battle to register myself as Ron Ranson Associates, and had to argue that I did in fact call in specialist people like photographers and lay-out artists on a regular basis. The registration fee will be £1, and, if you're accepted, you are issued with a Certificate of Registration which you should put in a prominent position in your office. It makes sense, therefore, not to go to the expense of having your stationery printed or making an entry in the telephone directory, until you know that the name you've chosen is going to be acceptable.

Now you've decided on your name or title let's talk about your stationery and literature; in other words, your corporate image. You all know of the corporate images produced by the big national and international companies such as the air lines, British Rail, British Petroleum, Shell and Unilever which spend millions co-ordinating their colour schemes and logos on everything from letterheads to delivery vans. It makes their organisations instantly recognisable to everybody. However, there isn't any reason at all why you, too, shouldn't adapt the same principle on a smaller scale in your own one man business. With good taste and possibly the services of a local graphic designer or enlightened printer, you can quickly begin to create your own house-style. This was the service I offered to small factories and businesses when I lost my job as publicity manager. Normally, the stationery a small firm accumulates in an ad hoc way. A little printer round the corner knocks up a letterhead quickly, perhaps another firm prints the business cards in a different typeface, and the subsequent literature often bears no overall resemblance at all, and each leaflet ends up looking as if it had been published by a different firm.

What is usually needed is a simple but strong overall design scheme which is adaptable enough to fit all your future needs. Decide on an appropriate typeface for the name, and stick to it throughout, together with a colour

Below: My son Lance's logo and stationery

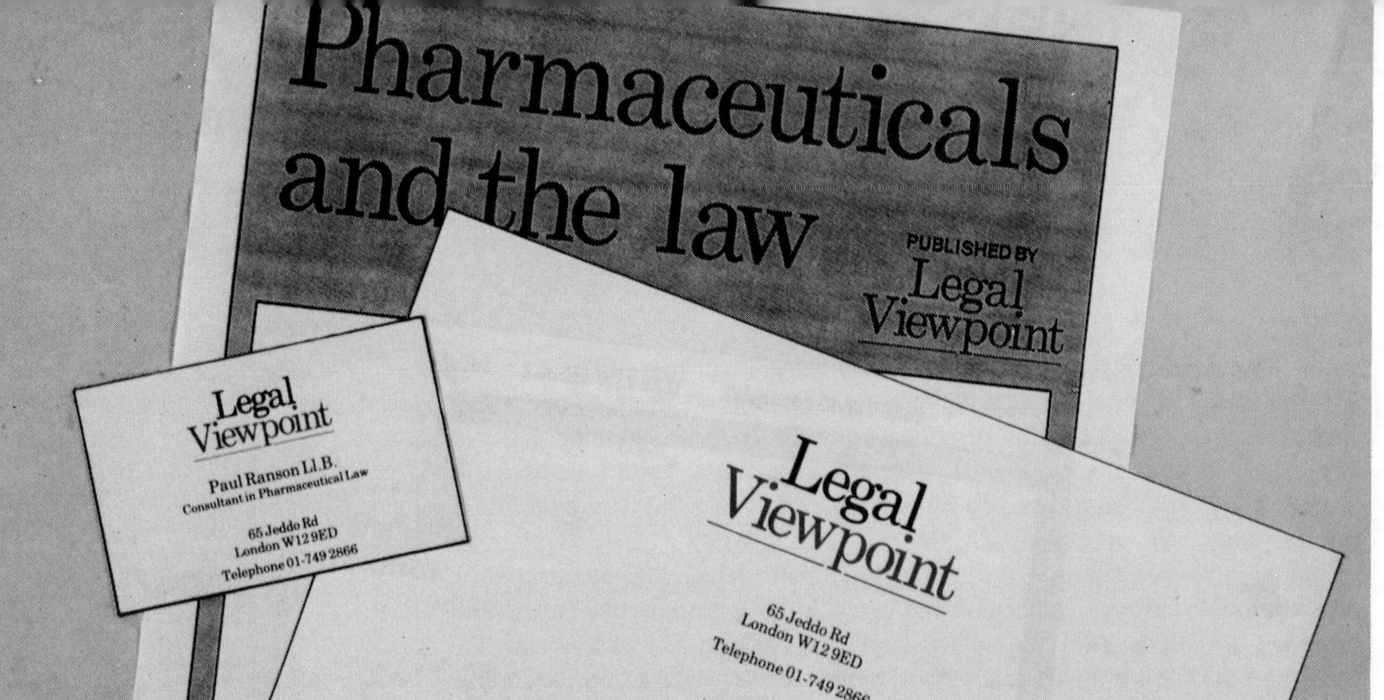

Above: My son Paul's stationery and monthly publication

scheme. Don't get frightened – it doesn't have to be expensive. Good taste is the important thing. Remember, it doesn't cost a penny more to print well designed literature rather than badly designed stuff. Take your letterhead for example, it's almost impossible to over emphasise its importance. It's often the only contact a client may have with you, and from its design you can give the impression of an old-fashioned backstreet firm or a dynamic go-ahead company. Just think of some of the letterheads you've received in the past.

My two sons have followed my example, and recently decided to start their own businesses. So the first thing we did was to produce good letterheads and business cards, a few of which are shown below. Lance decided to have turquoise as his house colour and everything is printed in that colour. Paul, who is in the legal profession, decided that black and grey would be more appropriate. Fortunately, colour continuity is now made easier because of a system called Pantone which lists an enormous range of colours and tints under numbers. Therefore, when you've decided on a colour, you can quote that particular number to any printer and get the identical shade. For example, Lance's turquoise is Pantone 313, and the grey which Paul uses is Pantone 436.

Public relations   This is very important in business but first let's define what is meant by PR. It's a way of presenting yourself and your product in a very favourable light to your customers or potential customers, at little or no cost. That's where it differs from publicity, which costs money but to a certain extent the two go hand in hand.

In publicity you take an advertisement or produce a leaflet, and you know for certain that you'll get what you pay for. In PR, however, you're using your wits and flair to tempt the media into giving you free mentions purely by making yourself newsworthy. If you succeed, the results will usually have much more credibility to the reader or viewer than any advertisement. If, for example, you were going to buy a new car you'd take much more notice of the editorial test reports in certain magazines than you would of the company advertisements. Once you know the basic rules of the game there are endless possibilities, and done consistently it can often make the difference between a business just plodding along and being a runaway success. Start by writing down what you want to achieve through PR. Such as establishing your identity firmly in your local community or making your name synonomous with paperclips, Bath buns or whatever. My own object is to make local people automatically think of me when they want a painting of the district, and on a more national basis I want amateur painters to think of me when they want to select a watercolour course. Obviously the biggest benefit for you in PR is to boost sales and increase confidence in your product or service, but it can also be used to protest loudly if you think you have been unjustly treated by officialdom.

The main targets for PR are the press, radio and television, but probably most of your dealings will be with the press so let's start there. Your local paper will usually be your main weapon, so first find out as much as you can about its basic character. Is it lively or sober? Does it like a good scandal? Does it carry plenty of news about your sort of business? Building up this understanding will help you find out what type of story the editors are looking for and your objective is to try to adapt your own items to fit their requirements. People usually think that you have to go cap in hand to get an editorial mention and that the newspaper will only give you one if you take an advertisement. The truth is that most local newspapers are crying out for news to fill their pages every week. The advertising and editorial departments are quite separate with different jobs to do anyway and they don't even have much contact with each other. The main secret to getting press coverage is convincing the paper that what you're doing is newsworthy – something cheaper, dearer, bigger, more original or in some way different from the ordinary run of events. If you present your information to the editor in an interesting and business like way and also in plenty of time to meet his press date, he's usually only too pleased to use it. The proper way is to prepare a press release. This means that you write your story in a certain way using some very basic rules. First, you try to think of a good headline. This is very important. It must be short, pithy, and newsworthy. This is a sort of bait which either makes the journalist look at the whole story or throw it in the waste paper basket. For instance, for a recent exhibition I held in Luxembourg the headline read 'Local Artist's Personal Export Drive'. The first paragraph should then contain the whole story in brief, written, of course, in the third person just as if a reporter had interviewed you. The next few paragraphs should fill in more of the details and some of the background material, which in my case was the success of the last exhibition and some details about the famous personality who was going to open the show. Put some information in quotes – newspapers love quotes. If this is well written and typed with double-line spacing, the chances are that the whole thing will be sent to the compositors intact. The main thing to remember is not to make exaggerated claims or to use superlatives. Just imagine yourself as the reporter writing it down. A good clear photograph attached to the press release is also useful. Measure the current column width of your local paper and trim your photograph to fit either one or two columns. In fact everything you do to make life easier for the editorial staff will pay dividends. At the bottom of the press release always put 'for further information contact . . .', and put your own name, address and telephone number. This often brings the newspaper back to you asking for more details. Of course if you can get on christian name terms with your local editor, so much the better.

Another type of publication, which has appeared on the scene recently and still growing fast, is the free sheet which is pushed through your letterbox whether you like it or not. It's usually produced by very few people and it relies entirely on selling advertisement space. They usually welcome any news item as their editorial staff is at a minimum, but you must be fair and advertise with them as well. If you want to get at the more well-to-do people in your district then aim for the county magazines. They may seem full of hunt-balls and golf-club matters but they do include the local business scene and they're always in need of editorial material.

Another idea is to produce your own newspaper which is exactly what I've done. At first, mine started off as a duplicated typed sheet giving details of next year's courses and prices, but after seeing my local garage's efforts I decided to write and produce an annual four page newspaper with items covering painting holidays abroad, exhibitions, even little stories about our own cats and dogs, together with course details and coupons for obtaining my book and video. Written in an informal and chatty way I am able to get many different messages over. People also seem to read it much more carefully than they would a leaflet, and it even seems to give them a sense of belonging to a club. A newspaper is very reasonable in terms of cost and your local printer will only be too glad to help you produce it – mine has a postal circulation of about 3,000 and I distribute at least another 3,000 at demonstrations.

Now to the national press. The same principles apply, but you're in a different league here and the chances of getting your press release accepted are very much smaller; in fact for the small business you're probably much better off concentrating on the local press, particularly if your activities are within a restricted area. However, if you need to attract customers nation-wide, have a go at the national press – you've nothing to lose.

What really brings results, though, are the magazines and there are literally thousands of them connected with trade, business, sport, art, DIY, hobbies, and cars, but, how do you find the right ones for your particular product or service? Start by going to your local library and looking through *British Rate* and *Data* (BRAD) or *Willing's Press Guide.* You'll soon have a list of all the relevant publications to your business field. Go out and buy a copy of each one to find out what sort of items they use, in other words, study them just as you did the local papers earlier. For example in my own particular narrow field there are two main publications, *The Artist* and the *Leisure Painter. The Artist* has a high proportion of professionals so it's a little up-market for me, *Leisure Painter* is right on the nose and all its 20,000 readers are potential customers. Therefore I not only advertise in it every month but regularly write articles on watercolour. This is where advertising and PR go hand in hand. The articles give credibility and the advertisements are the point of sale. The same applies whether you're making running shoes, lens hoods for cameras or a new type of gardening tool, there's a range of appropriate magazines just waiting for your press release if you present it the right way. To make PR work for you, you have to be constantly asking yourself every time you do something special in your business, 'How can I make this into a news item?'

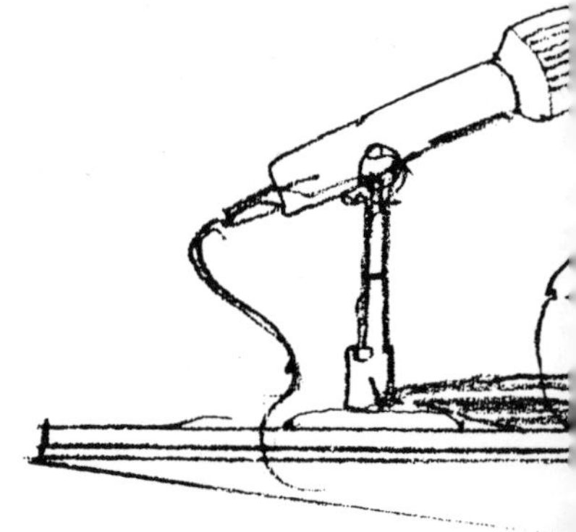

Let's now look at radio and television. The rewards for getting your message across on these are even greater than newspapers, but you're probably thinking by now that we're getting into the realms of fantasy for a one man business. In actual fact, local radio stations are hungry for news and are always looking for items of interest, so your chances of getting air-time are excellent. Begin as usual, by studying the various programmes objectively and pinpointing the ones that might be interested in your type of item. The people to contact are the researchers whose main job is to steer the rest of the team in the direction of good stories, fortunately news programmes have now discovered that 'industry' can be interesting. Local radio interviews are rather enjoyable. The atmosphere, is usually relaxed and casual, and disc jockeys seem to have an amazing knack of making you feel instantly at ease. Most of the interview is interspersed with music. The secret of success is to be intensely enthusiastic about your subject. Remember, they can't see your face so everything has to come through your voice.

Local television is fairly similar, and it is possible to get onto one of their local news programmes if you give them the right sort of press release as well as the right sort of visual potential. Sometimes they send a team around to your home, but usually interviews take place in their studios. As with radio, everyone including the interviewer will be very friendly. When you're on, look at the interviewer, never at the camera, otherwise it will seem contrived and it'll probably be the wrong camera anyway. The most important thing, though, is to be enthusiastic and sincere all the time, the rest will follow naturally.

Lecturing This is another form of PR and costs you nothing – you may even get paid for it.

What more could someone in business ask than to be invited by a group of people to talk and demonstrate your product, without interruption. What's more you have every salesman's dream, a captive audience. Just think of the advantages. It brings you and your product to the notice of a wide public and hopefully establishes you as an authority in your particular field. And communication works both ways, it broadens your own understanding of your potential customers, and helps you find out what makes them tick. However, the thought of standing alone in front of an audience and talking can scare the daylights out of many people.

I had all the usual signs of a beginner when I gave my first lecture to a class of would-be advertising executives – a dry throat, sweaty forehead and a hesitant manner and spent most of the time looking down at my notes. Somehow I got through the evening but it taught me how not to do it. The secret is to be completely relaxed if you possibly can. I know it's easier said than done when you're feeling scared inside, but the more experience you get, the more confident you'll become. This confidence gives you a more relaxed attitude which puts your audience at ease. Once you get the hang of it you begin to enjoy the whole game. You're given a lovely crowd of people you've never met before to play with, to amuse and interest, and afterwards you'll hopefully drive off into the night on a tide of goodwill. It's all very heady stuff and does wonderful things to your all round self-confidence. But how do you start? Well, audiences aren't hard to find. Women's Institutes, Professional Women's Guild, Rotary Clubs, Luncheon Clubs, Round Tables, Young Farmers Clubs, photographic societies, professional bodies and lots of others are all searching for lively speakers to talk on interesting topics, so all you have to do is contact the club secretaries and offer your services.

There's bound to be an interesting angle to your business, whether you're a chimney-sweep, hairdresser, picture framer or photographer, and you must have the makings of at least one good talk in you. My own effort is called 'The Excitement of Watercolour' and the same basic theme has been used for about 200 lectures and demonstrations. You won't 'win 'em all'. Sometimes you'll turn out on a wet night and have only a tiny audience who are very hard work. On other occasions though, they'll pack the room enthusiastically. Don't get the impression that I'm a 'natural' at this game, I've had to work hard at it, but perhaps I can pass on some of the practical tips.

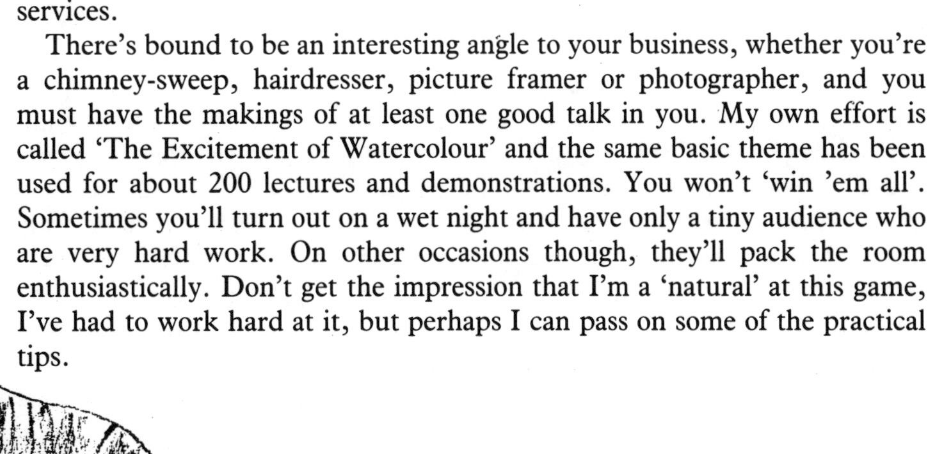

Whilst a talk is a good sales opportunity, it only works if it's kept low-key and objective, so don't try to ram your product down their throats. The main aim is to be informative, entertaining and modest; try to put yourself over as a friendly, honest and humorous person. As you gain experience, you'll be able to recognise instinctively the moment when you have your audience on your side. From then on it's fairly easy. Talking in public is a skill that has to be learned, and perhaps the best exponents are the stand-up comedians, many of whom have learned their business in the northern working men's clubs, they know all the tricks of how to capture the attention of an audience and keep that attention. The key to your success on the night is doing your homework beforehand. Find out from the organisers as much about your potential audience as you can. How many people there are likely to be, their main interests, the sort of speeches they're used to and how long they want you to speak for. Usually half an hour is enough. With this information, the next stage is to write the speech itself. Start by jotting down all the main points you want to get over. Just as they come into your head and then rearrange them in a logical order. Be careful about jokes. If they fall flat it can be embarrassing for both you and your audience. But humour is often a good way of getting over a serious point. You can choose humorous anecdotes, preferably about yourself, which seems to put them on your side and stops you from appearing too pompous. People also seem to enjoy having gentle fun poked at themselves.

Another important ingredient is brevity – don't waffle . Keep your sentences short, sharp and simple and never use long words when short ones will do. Probably the best way is to type out the key sentences, otherwise you'll spend most of your time reading your script with your eyes down when you should be looking at your audience. Always leave plenty of space between the lines, this makes it easier to find your place, and underline the key words you want to stress. My own way is to use just one sheet of paper and glance down at it casually if I get a bit stuck. In any case don't rely too much on your notes. Practise your speech several times beforehand on your husband or wife or use a tape recorder, which is useful not only for timing, but also for showing up irritating phrases and verbal mannerisms you may not have realised existed, such as 'you know' repeated about ten times.

The next thing is to case the joint, as the burglars call it. Go along to the room or hall and have a good look round. Find out what the seating is like and if you can be seen easily. Also whether or not you'll need a 'mike' and whether the table from where you're speaking is high enough for you to read your notes, or perhaps you'll need to hold them. These may seem small points, but they often make the difference between a first rate performance and a bit of a shambles. Having said this, a lot of places where I visit are a long distance away and often I arrive after a hundred mile journey and walk straight into an audience-filled room. However, I do try, if possible, to get there a good half hour before the time due, so that I can set my equipment out, and quietly get the feel of the place. One thing you'll probably never be able to avoid completely is nerves. Everybody has them a bit beforehand. You may feel you're quivering inside and your hands are shaking, but believe me, the audience won't notice half as much as you think and anyway the butterflies usually disappear as soon as you get going. Even experienced actors get nerves, and in reality they do actually help to keep your performance level up, and the adrenalin flowing. However, don't try to take 'dutch courage' in the local pub beforehand, as the combination of nerves and booze can be disastrous. When you're actually speaking, use your notes only when you have to and the rest of the time keep your eyes on your audience, fixing different areas for a few seconds at a time. This makes each member of the audience think you're looking straight at her when in fact your eyes are taking in a group of people. Don't talk too quickly. Nerves tend to make you talk faster than you normally do. Pronounce your words clearly and deliberately, and talk at a slower pace than usual. At one lecture the organiser said to me, 'You will speak up won't you. A lot of the ladies are rather old and deaf.' With these words in my ears I probably gave one of my best talks ever.

Often, another advantage is that you can put up a display of your literature and products at the back of the hall and sell them at the end of the evening, but be sure that the organisers are agreeable to this beforehand. I've sold hundreds of my books this way.

Advertising Now we've come to something you'll have to pay for. The skill involved here is to pinpoint your media in order to get the maximum effective publicity for each pound you spend – any fool can get publicity if he spends enough money.

Which medium you choose will depend very much on the nature of the product or services you offer, and of course how much you can afford. If your potential customers are local, if perhaps you're a hairdresser, a florist or a plumber, your options range from a postcard in a local shop, *Yellow Pages*, advertisements in local papers and 'free-sheets', or even a spot on local radio.

Don't shrug off a postcard in a shop window as it can be very effective if it's approached in a professional way. Don't scribble a hasty message, but treat it as a proper advertisement. Word it carefully and Letraset it if necessary with possibly a picture of what you're selling. If it's on coloured card, so much the better – in fact anything that will make it stand out from the rest will pay dividends. Supermarkets often have noticeboards near their entrances where you can advertise free. Don't just do one, either, but find half a dozen shops in the area and saturate them.

If you want an entry in *Yellow Pages*, the first thing you should do is ring up your local telephone operator and ask to be put through to *Yellow Pages* advertising department. If you have a business telephone line you can have one entry free under your own choice of heading, after that you pay for extra entries, and also for display advertisements. Obviously some types of businesses are more appropriate; you would, probably, be much more likely to choose a taxi firm through *Yellow Pages* than a travel agent.

Newspapers and magazines have already been mentioned earlier but it's worth repeating. The cheapest advertisement is in the classified section. It doesn't catch the eye, but simply lies in wait for someone looking for that particular service or product, and so it has to appear regularly to be effective. If you decide on a display advertisement, talk to someone in the advertising department of the newspaper and discuss it – they'll probably even design it for you too, but you may find it better to get a good local studio to do it. Go cautiously at first as they'll probably try to talk you into signing up for quite a few advertisements with promises of series discounts; do make sure of the response first. As with the postcards, the trick is to try and make your advertisement stand out from the 'herd'. If, however, you're hoping to sell by mail order or if your potential customers are scattered nationwide, you'll need to advertise in national newspapers and magazines. Although here you're in a bit of a jungle with literally hundreds of publications to choose from. It sounds daunting, but by first pinpointing your potential customer you can soon narrow down the field. For example, if you're selling a skimpy bra you'd not only choose the women's pages of newspapers and women's magazines, but you'd also make sure that the readers of the particular publication were in the right age and class group by reading through the magazine first to see at whom the editorial and other advertising is directed.

You have to be much more selective when you're actually paying good money, than when you're trying to get free PR. As I mentioned before, take a trip to the local library to see a copy of the *British Rate and Data* and find

out the relevant publications. The correct choice of the national daily and Sunday papers is also tricky, but they do each have strong differences in their readership, and I can't resist repeating something my son swears he saw on a lavatory wall at Gray's Inn.

Above: My own newspaper, brochure and advertisements

> 'The Times is read by the people who run the country,
> The Guardian is read by the people who think they run the country,
> The Financial Times is read by the people who own the country,
> The Mail is read by the wives of the people who own the country.

The Express is read by the people who want the country to be run in the way it was 40 years ago,
The Telegraph is read by the people who think it is run in the way it was 40 years ago,
The Mirror is read by the people who want the country to be run by someone else,
The Morning Star is read by the people who want the country to be run by another country,
and, the Sun and Star are read by the people who don't care who runs the country as long as she's got big tits!'

In other words you wouldn't try to sell a Bentley in the *Daily Mirror*, or a frying pan in the *Financial Times*. Also, when an advertisement tells you to reply to, say, Department HG3 it doesn't mean that they have lots of different departments, it just means that they want to find out how many replies they get from an advertisement in the March issue of *House & Garden* – try a similar code in your own advertisements.

Be wary of being too ambitious with your advertising initially, and make sure you've got adequate stock. A business in Oxfordshire had quietly progressed for years until they put one advertisement in a national magazine and were suddenly swamped with orders; they had to go into liquidation as their administration and production were quite unable to cope with the sudden demand. When you get into this league of advertising you'll need professional help to make your advertisements stand out from your competitors. Plenty of small advertising agencies are shown in the *Yellow Pages*, or you can get a list from the IPA (address at the back of this book). Agencies will advise you on the right choice of media, design and write the advertisement and book the space. Be sure to have a good look at their work first, and also find out their costs before you take them on. If the goods you're selling are to other firms rather than to individuals, you'll need to advertise in the trade press, and there are plenty of trade magazines whatever your trade. The same rules about careful selection apply here too.

When it comes to literature, unless you've had a lot of experience with print, leave the designing to a professional studio. Some printers have their own design departments, but don't trust a little local printer to do it, unless you've already seen some of his work. Good taste is far more important than money in preparing your literature. It's much better to get a well-designed leaflet in one or two colours on good quality paper than to lash out on full-coloured literature hastily produced on cheap paper. In fact the overall costs of both operations may even work out the same, as full colour means four runs through the machine and four expensive printing plates, but in the end it doesn't necessarily sell any better. You should try to get good crisp photography of your product in the beginning, this will form the basis of your literature. Estimating the print run is also important, because most of the cost of producing literature is in the origination and the plates or blocks and typesetting. A 2,000 print run will cost very little more than one of 1,500 once the machine is running, apart from the paper. Take care – you don't want to have an expensive re-run a month later but neither do you want stacks of literature collecting dust and which may become out of date, so be sure to get a firm estimate, beforehand, for alternative quantities. You'll be given a proof before the literature is printed, so check every word carefully before returning it. There's nothing worse than getting 5,000 finished copies with two or three spelling errors and a shrug of the shoulders from the printer.

Build up a mailing list of potential customers, but put the names in a card index rather than in a book, as you'll need to be constantly updating or cutting out 'dead wood'. My own system is very simple; when anyone makes an enquiry the name automatically goes on a card index with the date. If they subsequently attend one of the courses, a corner is cut off the card. Every year we send out our newsletter to about 3,000 names on the list. If we don't do any business with them after two years, the names are then removed to make room for more recent enquiries. Those with the corners cut off remain in the system. Sometimes organisations exchange lists or rent them out. An artists' book club and I send out each other's literature which practically doubles both our mailings without increasing our postage. There are also companies which will supply you with ready-made specialist mailing lists for a fee, for example the addresses of all the dentists in Wales, or the fish-mongers in Cornwall. By the way, if you're direct mailing for the first time, the post office offer special terms, they'll mail 1,000 first class postings, or 1,240 second class ones completely free. You can get more details from your local postal services representative, his number is in the telephone directory. If you're mailing locally, the electoral register is useful for individual customers and *Yellow Pages* for local firms. Leaflet distribution is a more modest version of direct mail. At its simplest it could be a leaflet pushed through 100 neighbourhood doors. Hard up, but reliable, teenagers may be glad to help you at an agreed rate. If you want to cover a larger or more distant area, some firms will deliver for you – look in the *Yellow Pages* under 'Sample and Circular distributors'.

Exhibitions can cover anything from taking a stall at your local agricultural show or 'Craft Fayre' to large trade fairs in big cities such as London and Birmingham. If you're just starting out, a local event is often a good way of gauging the public's reaction to your product, firsthand, without too much expense. This might apply even if your product is on the fringe of the event; for example, if you were developing a new polish you might demonstrate it at an antique fair, or if you were an artist specialising in cars you might produce a lot of interest and orders at a vintage rally. Moving upmarket, there are annual trade fairs and exhibitions for practically every sector of commerce, from toys to health foods. They fulfil three basic functions; market research, selling your product and finding out what your competitors are up to. They can be expensive, both in money and time. If you're on your own you need to be there to demonstrate your product, distribute your literature and take down enquiries. Incidentally, it's vital that these enquiries are quickly and efficiently followed up or your money will be wasted. You may feel that while you're there you're not actually producing anything; however, you should at least get your expenses back in the long run as well as gaining valuable information and contacts. My

younger son, Lance, for example, who has just started up his own one man greetings card publishing business feels it's vital that he appears at the annual Gift Fair at the National Exhibition Centre, where trade buyers from all over the country come to consider and purchase their next year's range. It also keeps him up to date with new ideas and developments. If you can't afford a whole stand, you might be able to share one with another firm making a related product, or organise a joint venture with one of your suppliers. If you do decide to exhibit, try and write to your potential trade buyers by name beforehand, together with your literature and your stand number and invite them for a chat.

I've described some of the varying techniques available for promotion, but they do work most effectively when they're interlocking. Perhaps I can explain that better by running over my own strategy. I advertise regularly in the *Leisure Painter*, putting in a different painting each month to attract attention, but keeping the same copy. This brings a steady stream of enquiries which are sent a brochure and a newsletter giving dates of courses and vacancies. It's important to send them off by return so that your prospect doesn't have a chance to lose interest. I also give about five lectures a month around the country where more literature is distributed. This is all backed up by press releases to the local papers and art magazines when anything exciting happens, together with occasional painting articles in *Retirement* and other magazines. Another thing I've done is to hang my pictures in the bank and in my doctor's and dentist's waiting rooms, changing them around periodically. Of course, when a book comes out, everything goes into top gear and the publishers arrange up to fifteen radio and television interviews in one week around the launch date. The main message here is continuity. Keep plugging away on all fronts and try, constantly, to think of new ideas.

Chapter 7

Calling in the Experts

By now you will have seen that if you do set up in business you may have to be your own designer, do your own PR, be your own buyer and lots of other things besides, but one of the worst mistakes you could make is to fool yourself that you can do *everything*. There are trained professionals around you, and it's false economy to try and rely on your own judgement and opinions all the time. The fees charged by them can be set legitimately against tax and others are ready to help you for practically nothing.

Bank Manager He should be the first person you approach about your intended business venture, even if it's still only on the horizon. There's a right and wrong way of of approaching him. Don't just wander in on the off-chance with your figures written on the back of an envelope – it won't exactly inspire his confidence in you. You should make an appointment, but before this you should have put a lot of time and thought into presenting your proposition.

The manager will want to know what your idea is and to see a realistic budget forecast, what you have to spend out, and what you expect to receive in payments. He'll also want to know how long it will be before you hope to break even or show a profit. You'll then be asked what securities you can offer against the loan; these might be insurance policies, even the deeds to your house if you own it, or a second mortgage if it is still mortgaged. It's not just the finance he'll want to discuss with you, but he'll need to be assured that you've got the appropriate experience or, if you're breaking new ground, that your research has been thorough. Usually, you'll only get a loan if you're prepared to put some of your own money into the business as well.

Put your case over factually but in an enthusiastic way. Don't cover anything up, tell the whole story honestly, giving both the good and the bad features – if you don't you'll certainly be found out. It's a hard fact, but banks won't bail you out if you get into trouble, they're only really interested in success stories. Sometimes it's better to ask for overdraft facilities rather than a loan because the charges are usually less. Don't necessarily expect an instant decision as your bank manager will need a few days to do his homework.

From the moment you finally get your overdraft or loan, make your bank manager your constant adviser and confidant. Keep an eye on your budget forecast and if it has to be revised, go and see him and explain the reasons. Always be one step ahead of him. Never make him have to telephone you first. If you know your account is going to be stretched more than you thought, tell him why beforehand. Make a habit of keeping in touch at least every three months or so, or more frequently if your business is going through a sticky patch. Bank managers don't like silences. I've always made a point of getting on christian name terms with mine, even asking him up for drinks occasionally. It's not crawling, it's just common sense. Finally, you should be aware that your high street bank, through its subsidiaries, also offers you various other useful services such as insurance, import/export, foreign exchange facilities, computer services and equipment leasing services. But there is more of this in the next chapter.

Accountant   Good accountants can save you a lot of money, often many times their fees. However, just like solicitors, they specialise, and you'll need to find one who is particularly knowledgeable on the financial aspects of self-employed people. He should be aware not only of all the hazards and pitfalls but also the possibilities and advantages. Also, as you have a small business it's obviously better to go to a small sized firm with a knowledge of local conditions and personalities rather than a large city company with many partners where you would probably be fobbed off with one of the juniors.

Being a complete coward with figures, I've employed an accountant to deal with my tax forms on Schedule D ever since I started freelance work to supplement my full time job many years ago. Over the years I have been constantly amazed at all the completely legitimate claims that he manages to get agreed with the tax authorities. I've had an absolute treasure of an accountant for the last ten years who is the most honest man I know, and yet he seems to take a personal pride in cutting my tax bill to the bone. Letters and counter-letters fly backwards and forwards between my accountant and the tax authorities culminating in quite a modest demand in the end. Also, the tax authorities seem to trust accountants more than they do an individual because of their professional integrity. I do urge you strongly not to hide things from your accountant, but to lay everything on the table and let him do the worrying and the arguing legitimately. Of course you have to pay the accountant's fees which are usually charged on an hourly basis according to the type of work. There are no fixed charges. Therefore, let him know, preferably in writing, what you want him to do, such as filling in tax returns, doing the VAT, giving advice on book-keeping, and ask what the charges are likely to be, and his bill will then be itemised.

Solicitors   It's always better to find a solicitor before you actually need one. Don't hesitate to shop around. Interview one or two until you find one with whom you can establish a rapport. If you openly admit that you're seeing other solicitors, before deciding, they'll probably meet you for about quarter of an hour without charge; in fact they'll probably be glad of a chance to size you up as well.

It's advisable to try to find one that specialises in business matters, rather than in divorce or conveyancing. As a small business, you'll probably get more personal attention from a small firm of solicitors, and personal recommendations are always worth following up. When you finally decide on a solicitor suitable for your business needs never sign any document or commit yourself to any agreement without consulting the solicitor first. He understands all the small print on a contract and why it's there and he's also in constant contact with banks, businesses and local authorities so will be able to provide practical advice and useful introductions to help solve your problems. As there are some blurred areas covered by both solicitors and accountants it's a good idea to get the two together at an early stage so that they can chew over any problem with the minimum waste of time and thus avoid duplications.

Members of Parliament Knocking your MP seems to be a national pastime. But to be fair, MPs do quite a lot of work behind the scenes for their constituents with problems. They regularly hold 'surgeries' which are advertised in the local paper, and if you feel you're a victim of some misjustice or unfairness, such as being refused planning permission, it may well be worth attending one of these 'surgeries' and asking your MP to take up the cudgels on your behalf.

Your MP is able to approach the ministry responsible for your troubles and even in extreme cases to ask a question in the House of Commons. Although your MP mustn't be seen to take sides, things can be stirred up a bit for you in order to cause a bit of bureaucratic squirming. You can write to your MP, by name, at the House of Commons, London SW1A 0AA.

Government Departments Perhaps one of the most underused Government sponsored services, and one which was set up especially to help people like you and me, is The Small Firms Service sponsored in England by the Department of Trade and Industry. The Scottish and Welsh Development Agencies run their own, and in Northern Ireland it's called The Local Enterprise Development Unit; you will find the address at the back of this book.

After the bank manager, these are the next people you should contact when you're thinking of starting up on your own – they'll even pay for your call if you dial 100 and ask the operator for Freephone 2444. You'll be sent a

range of leaflets about the services they offer and on various aspects of running a business. They have eleven regional centres around England alone, so there should be one fairly near you. One of their most useful functions is to put you in touch with a whole range of specialist advisers ranging from the appropriate people in government departments, local authorities and chambers of commerce, to professionals in accounting, law, property, finance and exporting. They're a very enthusiastic bunch of civil servants who will try and help you as much as possible, but if they cannot they'll pass you to another group: The Small Firms Counselling Service which has some fifty counselling offices around the country. These offices are run by advisers who are very experienced business people; some may still be in business and some may be retired. The first counselling session is free and the charge for subsequent sessions, which are limited to ten days in any one year, is modest and very good value for money.

If you're starting up in a country district try another group called the Council for Small Industries in Rural Areas (CoSIRA), discussed in more detail in the next chapter, which was established to help small businesses setting up in rural areas of England. Similar services are offered by the Development Board for Rural Wales, the Highland and Islands Development Board and the Scottish Development Agency. They're all interested and anxious to help new starters once the business is going, and they can provide business training and financial advice. There are two other organisations running short courses for people starting up in their own businesses. The first one is a non-profit making company called URBED Enterprise Development that interviews you first to assess your suitability for their various programmes from an intensive one-week course to a twelve-week learning programme. They'll help you to create a business idea if you haven't got one and if you have, they'll convert your own idea into a feasible enterprise, and will then judge your prospects.

Finally there's The London Enterprise Agency which runs one-day courses for people starting their own businesses. Their one-day course will introduce the basic skills needed to start and run a business, including the financial side and the many sources of help available. They also run more advanced courses over four consecutive weekends.

Addresses for all these organisations are at the back of the book.

Book-keeper   This is another service which is usually charged on an hourly basis. In my business I employ a book-keeper on a part-time basis and she comes in for a few hours each month. She is actually a housewife who did a lot of this sort of work in her past job. I pass over the month's bank statement and cheque books, paid bills and paying-in slips and within about three or four hours she has the lot sewn up. It's a good idea to let the accountant tell you exactly how the accounts are to be itemised from the beginning so that when the books are passed over at the end of the year he has all the information needed.

Local libraries Never forget your local library. It's not just there to provide the latest Barbara Cartland romance. Librarians are trained professionals in the art of finding out information on any subject without delay. Why struggle along alone when they could be doing the job for you much more efficiently?

A good reference library has a wealth of information on *your* business and a range of directories covering practically everything. You won't be able to take out the directories, but most libraries have facilities, on the premises for photo-copying anything you may need. When I was doing research for this book my own library was very helpful, the staff seemed to take a personal interest and lent me armfuls of reference books. Don't forget to renew your books – by 'phone if necessary. The fines have been increased a lot recently.

Chapter 8

Money Matters

The first thing you must do is to sit down and work out how much money you'll need to begin your business. This is called your 'start-up capital' and will be tied into the business permanently. It's money which has to be laid out before you've made a single item or dealt with a single customer. The capital required will vary vastly depending on what sort of business you're proposing.

If you're going to hire out your skills and knowledge as a freelance working from home, it may only be the cost of a typewriter or drawing board, but on the other hand, it may involve renting or buying new premises with machinery, tools, office equipment, the installation of telephone and other services. If you're buying an existing business you'll also have to pay for the 'goodwill'. There are also hidden costs, like the legal fees, survey fees

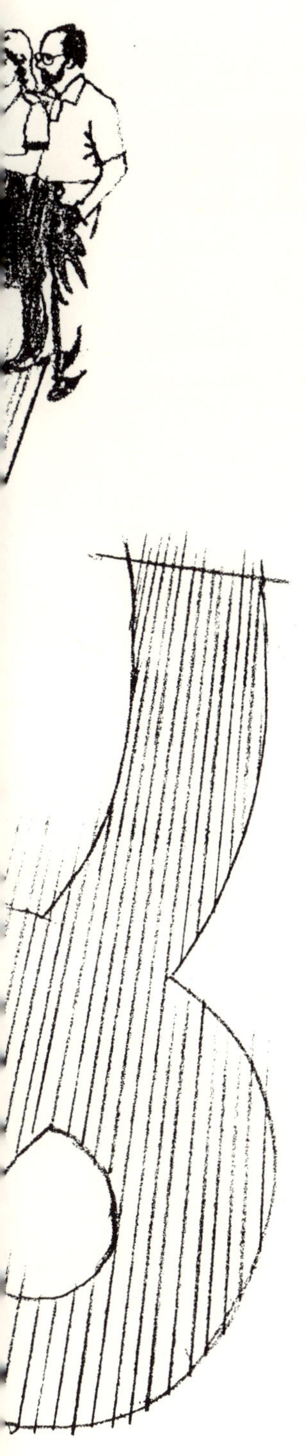

and accounting fees. Even stationery can be an expensive item. Finally the publicity; this is a vital factor for a new business. Once all this has been calculated you then have to add on the probable running expenses to keep the business going, until the money starts to roll in. This will include money you'll need to live on as well as to pay your rent or mortgage, rates etc.

The next step is to draw up an appropriate cash-flow forecast for the first year of business. This is the amount of money that you envisage flowing in and out of the business from month to month. It will usually be uneven due to various factors, sometimes seasonal; for example, if you're making beach balls or Christmas decorations. Your overheads too will have to be paid unevenly, rates will probably come in twice a year, telephone and electricity every quarter. You may even get lots of bills one month and none at all the next. So, in making your cash-flow forecast add everything up for the year and then divide by twelve in order to work out each month's outgoings. This forecast will give you a fair idea of how much actual money you will need for the first year.

Where to get your capital   There are two sources of money, your own and borrowing. The ratio between your own funds and what you have to borrow is called the 'gearing of the business'. It's highly geared if the level of loans is high compared with your own funds. If you've put more money in than borrowed, the business is low geared. Lenders don't like this ratio to be too high because it makes their loans more risky. Normally they expect you to put up at least half the amount.

Obviously, the first place to go to for a loan is the bank. They make their profit by lending money so they will welcome your business providing they're not going to lose by it. It's probably best to send your bank manager a letter first asking for an interview. This gives the manager time for consideration and to find out how you've conducted your account in the past and also to make a few enquiries about the kind of business you propose. Go well prepared with all the facts. State how much money you want, why you want it, when you want it and how you propose to repay it together with the interest. He'll want to know of all your existing overdrafts, mortgages, and loans, with confirmation of the details given and the soundness of your predictions. He will also want to see your cash-flow forecast, as it will help him make sure that you're asking for enough money. This may sound strange, but many people in new businesses are much too modest in their requirements and forget to make provisions for slack times and unforeseen disasters. If in doubt, ask for more money rather than less. If the bank provides you with a loan it is sharing the risk of your possible failure. It must, therefore, protect itself by demanding security in the form of assets. These may be personal insurance, endowment policies or your own home if it's freehold or on a long lease. This may sound a little rash, but the banks have a right to expect your own stake, in effect, to equal theirs. However, the Department of Trade has set up a Small Business Loan Guarantee Scheme to help would-be businesses by guaranteeing 80% of the loan so long as it's not over £75,000. Though you will be required to pledge all your business assets as security.

Banks can lend money to you in two different ways. They can agree on an overdraft which is probably the cheapest form of finance as the interest rate is set by the manager himself, depending on the probable risk involved. The snag here is that because of possible government credit limits in the future, some or all of the credit can be called back at short notice. This should therefore be regarded as short-term finance, and you should expect to pay it off as soon as possible. The other method is by a fixed term loan. This is on a fixed rate of interest for about five years and may be at a higher rate of interest than an overdraft. If, after all this, your bank manager turns you down, don't despair. Try some of the other high street banks and ask about their schemes to help those starting businesses.

Another source of long term loan may be your family or friends. A new government sponsored Business Expansion Scheme means that those investing up to £40,000 in a small company may be able to deduct the whole amount against their taxable income. For businesses on their way – the minimum investment is £5,000 – ICFC may be another source of financial help. Owned jointly by the Bank of England and the clearing banks, it has an excellent record as a sleeping partner offering outstanding advice.

If you're setting up in business where the government is trying to encourage employment, such as in development areas and enterprise zones, you'll probably be able to obtain a regional development grant. As mentioned in the previous chapter, if you're basing your business in a rural area – and this includes country towns with up to 10,000 inhabitants – you may be able to get a loan from the Council for Small Industries in Rural Areas (CoSIRA). The minimum loan is £250 and the maximum is £75,000. However, it never puts up more than half the cost of any particular project. The Department of the Environment also makes grants or loans to encourage industry back into parts of the urban areas of major cities.

Costing   Your product or service must be costed realistically as this is a vital factor in your business set up. First you've got to establish a break-even point by combining a number of different factors; if you underestimate this you may find you're making a loss rather than a profit.

Making and selling a product   The factors to be added here are basically, raw materials if you're manufacturing, or your stock if you're selling, plus all your overheads which should include rent and rates, heating and lighting, advertising, travel expenses, car depreciation, telephone, printing, stationery and everything else you can think of! These calculations should be made for a set period, such as a year. You then divide this figure by the number of product units you expect to sell annually. For example, if you make 5,000 of a product and the total of your materials plus overheads comes to £15,000, your break even point is £3, to which you must add your intended profit margin. If you charge £5 each for the product, you should in theory make £10,000 per year.

Giving a service   Here the idea is the same, though obviously the overheads will be the major factor. Therefore, every expense including travelling time, car depreciation, insurance, petrol and other things will have to be included. This total annual figure must be divided by the number of hours a year you estimate you will be working and charging for. For example, if your overheads are £7,500 and you will be charging 1,500 hours annually you'll need to charge £5 per hour, just to break even. If you actually charge your clients £9 per hour, you should, in theory, make £6,000 profit per year. Having said all this, it's still a question of 'supply and demand'. You might be able to charge more than you thought, or less. It depends on the scarcity value of your service, that's why dentists earn more than labourers. In the end, arriving at a realistic price will only come with experience, based on past records and the knowledge of what the market will bear.

Getting paid   This, believe it or not, is quite an important part of your business and you should get to know a few of the 'tricks' of the game.

In hard times such as these, businesses, even large and reputable ones, tend to pay their bills slowly. The trick seems to be to collect what is owed to you as quickly as possible and to delay paying your own bills for as long as your creditors will let you. It's a recognised way of running a business without having to borrow so much from the bank. Unless you're paid cash on delivery, have your invoices printed with your business name, address, 'phone number and the word 'Invoice' at the top, with your paying terms eg '30 days after delivery'. You should write in the date, description of the item and the price. Also if you're registered for VAT this should be shown separately with your VAT number printed too. Each invoice should have a separate number for reference. Many firms don't pay until they receive a statement; these should be sent out each month with the word 'Statement' at the top listing all the invoices that haven't been paid, with their numbers and dates. You should have a duplicate of each invoice and statement you send out, and keep the copy invoices in a lever file and transfer them to another file when they've been paid. Each paid invoice should be checked against the statement, and those still unpaid must be repeated in the following month's statement.

If you're being paid personally by cheque, don't hesitate to ask to see a cheque card and write the card number, yourself, on the back of the cheque. Unless you know the person, don't accept a cheque for over the £50 limit guaranteed by the card. Even if the cheque bounces, keep it, because it's evidence of an agreed debt.

Not getting paid   If your payment hasn't materialised after sixty days, send a polite letter reminding them of your terms, and let them know how overdue the invoice is and ask if they have any reason for delaying payment. If you get no reply after another month, write again, giving them a deadline, perhaps unstamped so that at least the letter will be noticed. There will be times when you have to be fairly forceful and persistent about getting what is owed to you or you may find yourself at the back of the queue. If that fails, threaten legal action. Often a County Court Summons sent out leads to sudden payment. Keep a 'black list' of bad payers, and make sure you don't work for them again as they're just not worth the hassle.

Finally, bear in mind that bad debts can usually be claimed as a business expense on your income tax return.

Keeping the books   In any business, whether you're a potter or a plumber, your accounts are vital to the operation. Accounts are invaluable as a barometer of the health of your operations, quite apart from the fact that the Inland Revenue and VAT people will get very cross if you don't keep them properly. Accounts give you a chance to change direction and avoid financial pit-falls before they actually happen.

Juggling with figures may be completely alien to your nature, but try to summarise your accounts at the end of each month to make sure the past four weeks have been profitable and you'll have enough cash in hand for the operations next month. You should also ask the bank to send you monthly statements rather than quarterly. Although the basic principles of book-keeping are universal, every single business has its own individual needs which must be recorded and monitored regularly. By far the best thing, therefore, is to go to your accountant and describe all your business requirements, then let the accountant set the books up for you and teach you how to keep them. This will be money well spent, and the accountant will be only too pleased to do this for you as it will mean less work at the end of the year. After that, use your accountant only to keep you on the right track and to give you professional knowledge. Once your accounts have been set up you'll probably be able to do the actual day to day book-keeping yourself, in the evenings, or perhaps get someone else in the family to take on the task.

My accounts are actually done by a local woman who comes in once a month. The whole idea is to keep accounts to the absolute minimum and yet have basic information which you can quickly produce at any time. Your accountant will probably recommend that you keep four separate categories of records.

The first one is a cash book, this records all your payments out on the left side and all your receipts on the right. Secondly, an analysis book which itemises all your payments out into different categories, such as light and heat, bought-out services and materials etc. These can be obtained from your stationer with different numbers of vertical columns depending on how many classifications you require. This means you can easily check how much each of your expenses has amounted to. Their total will give you the whole month's costs. If you're VAT registered you'll also have to have another column for this, so that you can record how much VAT has been paid to you and how much you've paid yourself. You will need two arch files for your invoices to your customers and two more arch files for your suppliers and expenses. Arch files are loose-leaf covers with lever operated arches. You'll also need a paper punch to put the appropriate holes in the left-hand margins. The first file should be labelled, 'Customers Bills Unpaid', and the second 'Customers Bills Paid'. You will need two more files for your suppliers bills and expenses, label them, 'Bills Unpaid', and 'Bills Paid'. As you receive your bills, they are placed in the first file and when paid are transferred to the other file. You can, then, tell by looking at both unpaid files, how much money is owed to you and how much you owe at any specific time. You'll need a petty cash book for all the odd expenses like, taxis, teabags and tips. Cash items should be taken out of a float which is kept topped up regularly from the bank and a record of it made in the cash book. This book should be on the same lines as the analysis book with different columns for expenditure.

Apart from the books themselves you must keep evidence that the transactions you have recorded have actually taken place. You can do this in various ways; keep all your cheque book stubs together and make sure that you use the bank paying-in books, not just the odd slips – these usually get lost.

It doesn't matter how small your business, you should have separate accounts for business and private money. Bank statements will then show transfers of money from one account to the other, providing an authenticated record of money taken from the business as personal income or transferred, the other way round, as capital being introduced into the business.

This chapter is intended only as a simple guide to the financial basics of your business. There are several specialised books on the subject, which you'll find listed in the back of the book.

Chapter 9

Taxes – How to Lessen Them

First of all, a dire warning. When you're starting up a business on your own, don't for heaven's sake try to pretend the tax men aren't there on the principle of letting sleeping dogs lie. You might get away without paying tax for quite a long time, but when they eventually do catch up with you, you'll be in a lot of trouble. They can be very vicious in making you pay tax, with interest, on what *they* say – not what you think – was your profit since you started business, plus penalties which could even treble the sum.

There are all sorts of ways in which they find out about small businesses starting up. For example, its someone's job at the local tax office to read all the local papers to discover who's doing what and where. So many people seem to derive a strange satisfaction from sending anonymous letters to the authorities informing on their neighbours. Even worse, the Revenue and Customs have greater powers to check on premises and books than even the police. All in all, tax evasion is a criminal offence and not worth all the worry and anguish. Tax avoidance, however, is perfectly legal. Having warned you about all this, you are definitely in a much better tax position than an employee who pays PAYE and your opportunity to claim allowances is very much greater.

The first thing you should do, on deciding to become self-employed, is to tell your local Inspector of Taxes; you will find the address in your local telephone directory under the heading Inland Revenue. You will then be sent a pamphlet and a form 41G, which you must fill in and return. You should also let the DHSS know about your new status as a self-employed person for National Insurance purposes. Although this is covered in the next chapter on insurance, taxes and social security are linked because your Class 4 Insurance contributions are assessed together with your income tax by the Inland Revenue, and both are collected together. Once you're on Schedule D (as your new tax code is called) you may not need to pay any income tax for the first two years, but don't think that you're going to get away with any-

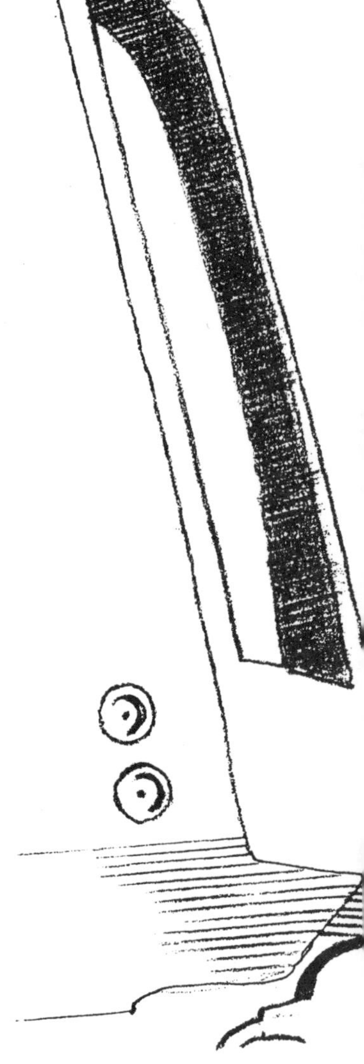

thing. When the business has been going for two whole tax years, the tax is charged on the preceding year basis. For example, your tax bill for 1985/6 will be on the profit you made in 1984/5. From then on it has to be paid in two equal instalments on 1 January and 1 July. One danger is that you may be tempted to spend the profits while you've got them and have no ready cash to pay the tax bill when it does finally come. It's a good idea, therefore, to get your bank to transfer a regular amount into a deposit account each month for future contingencies. The bank will pay you interest on it which, of course, has to be declared. One of the biggest advantages for the self-employed person is that you can claim relief for all expenses 'wholly and exclusively' incurred for your business. For example, under Schedule D you can claim for all your stationery, as an employee you couldn't even claim for a pencil.

It may be advantageous too, to take your wife or husband in as a partner, or even as an employee, if they're not already employed elsewhere. The tax men will probably want proof that your spouse is an active partner, so it's a good idea to have a written agreement drawn up. Also include their name on your stationery and make them a signatory on the business bank account. Here's a check list of the type of business expenses you'll normally get away with and a few you won't.

General running expenses Heating, lighting, telephone, rates, rent, window cleaning, office cleaning, postage, wrapping materials, stationery and typewriting repairs.

Working from home An allowance is made on a proportion of your rent and rates for the part of your house used exclusively for business purposes. Watch it though, as you'll have to be careful about capital gains tax when you sell your house. If you claim half the rates against tax it then means only half of the house is residential, with the other half being classed as commercial. When you sell the house, you'll be liable to pay capital gains tax on the appreciation of its value during that time. The tax will amount to half of the increase in actual value.

Wages and salaries Wages, salaries, and leaving payments to employees, payments to temporary staff, outworkers, pensions to ex-employees and their dependants, but not your own wages or salary or that of your partner(s). But if your wife helped you by taking telephone messages or acting as a part time assistant, you can pay her a wage allowed against tax. If it's less than £1,768 she won't need to pay tax or National Insurance stamps either because of a wife's earned income relief.

Stock All goods bought in for re-sale including raw materials and spare parts.

Travel Train fares, taxis, air travel, car hire, hotels, meals, gratuities, excess baggage charges and the running costs of your own car, but only a proportion of it if it's also used for private purposes.

Car You won't be allowed the actual cost of buying the car, but you'll probably be allowed the capital allowance on it.

Repairs All the normal repairs and maintenance to buildings and equipment, but you probably won't be able to claim on improvements or additions to the buildings.

Entertainment Entertainment of clients from overseas and your own costs while doing so, but you won't be able to claim for the business entertainment of clients from the UK.

Leasing and hire purchase The rent paid for leasing your equipment or car. The hire charge part of the payments (which is the amount you pay less the cash price), but not the price itself (see Capital allowances).

Professional fees Accountants fees, legal expenses, preparing service agreements, defending business rights, but you won't be allowed fines and other penalties for breaking the law or the cost of fighting a tax case, for instance.

Charges Bank charges, interest on overdrafts or loans for business purposes.

Publications Relevant books, newspapers, periodicals and other publications.

Subscriptions Professional societies, associations and trade organisations.

Taxes Purchase tax, selective employment tax, employer's contribution to National Insurance stamps, but not your own National Insurance stamps.

Provision for retirement The cost of your own and your partners' self-employed annuity.

Debts Specific bad debts, and partly doubtful debts, but you won't be able to claim for a general reserve for these purposes.

Insurance All industrial policies, such as public, product and employee liability, fire and theft, and vehicle insurance, but you won't be allowed to claim for your own life, health, or accident insurance.

Publicity Newspaper and magazine advertisement, sales literature, photography, promotional gifts, press and sales conferences, Christmas cards and calendars, promotional gifts, and payments to freelancers.

Capital allowances You can claim capital allowance for money spent on buying such things as, tables, chairs, office partitions, typewriters, calculators, cars, vans, drawing boards, machinery, musical instruments – in fact anything that has a long-term benefit for the business and doesn't need

renewing every year. The equipment itself is not tax deductible but allowances are given for the expenditure. It must be 'wholly and exclusively' for the business. For anything used partly for business and partly for private use, like a car, you get a portion of the capital allowances depending on the proportion of business use.

There are two aspects of capital allowance that must be understood: so you've got two things to be understood. Pool of expenditure, which is the total written down value of all equipment you claim capital allowance on, and writing down allowance, in which you can claim up to twenty-five per cent of your pool of expenditure at the end of each calendar year. If you sell something you've been claiming capital allowance on, the proceeds must be deducted from your pool of expenditure before working out your writing down allowance for the accounting year in which you sell it. The writing down allowance on a car costing more than £8,000 is restricted to a maximum of £2,000 in any year, and each car costing more than £8,000 or used partly for private purposes has its own separate pool of expenditure. There are special rules applying for capital allowances on buildings and it's best to check this with your tax inspector.

Inheritance tax   This is the tax on things you leave on your death. Your dependants are treated better by the taxman if you leave your money tied up in your own business, rather than in such things as houses or shares. The assets of a business, payable for inheritance tax are reduced by half – for a business worth £300,000 it would be valued for this purpose at £150,000. This makes a big difference, because if your children were left a £150,000 business rather than in shares etc. they would pay less than £4,000 rather than over £30,000. They would also have over eight years to pay, rather than one year, which applies to most taxable gifts, so it's easier to pay the tax gradually, without having to sell the business to do it.

Value added tax (VAT)   To most of us who are self-employed VAT is a nuisance and involves hours and hours of tedious paperwork, as you act as an unpaid tax collector for the government. On the other hand, it could be a financial advantage to you to register – even if you don't have to – particularly if you sell things abroad, supply businesses which are registered, or sell things which are zero rated for VAT. It doesn't, necessarily, affect you unless your turnover is over a certain amount, with the threshhold rising slightly with each budget. It is, I understand, hardly worth the effort of the Customs & Excise to collect the tax with a turnover under about £50,000, but our partners in the EEC insist upon it being levied.

You must register for VAT if your taxable turnover, which is the total value of goods and services you sell, exceeds £7,000 in the past three months, or £20,500 in the past year, or if your taxable turnover is likely to be more than £20,500 in the next year. Your first move is to contact your local Customs & Excise VAT office, the address is in your local telephone directory. They will then send you a form, VAT 1. It's essential not to delay this, because you're made to account for, and pay, any tax due from the date you first became liable and not from the date you actually notify them. If

you're late in informing them, you'll still be liable to pay the arrears of tax, even if you haven't charged VAT to your customers, and you will not be able to claim credit for the VAT you, yourself, have paid out. You're also likely to be confronted with heavy fines if you fail to register. You'll then be given a VAT registration number which will have to be included on all your invoices. A Customs & Excise officer will visit you to discuss your books and records and explain how to keep them as simple as possible, and also give you advice on how VAT affects you and generally be helpful about any problems you might have. After that, you'll be visited from time to time, normally with prior warning but not necessarily so, and your accounts checked in detail. There are all sorts of penalties for those who don't comply in every respect. There always seems to be something wrong, every time the officer lands on my doorstep, entirely, I must admit, due to my ignorance or poor arithmetic.

Once you're locked into the system, you'll have to pay the Customs fifteen per cent of the price you charge for supplying positively rated goods or services. You collect this from your customers either by showing the amount separately on your bills or including it in the total price. Even if you only give a service such as providing accommodation, catering, hairdressing or doing repairs, you still have to charge your clients. On your invoices you should give details of the VAT charges and also your VAT registration number. There are three categories of VAT rating:

1. Standard rating – fifteen per cent is charged, but liable to change at the government's whim.
2. Zero rated – which in theory, tax could be payable but isn't, for example, on books, food in shops and exported goods.
3. Exempt – in which VAT is never payable, for example, insurance and doctors' services.

Let me explain how VAT works in a simple but effective way. Imagine a chain of people – first the material producer, who sells his steel goods to the manufacturer charging VAT. The manufacturer claims the VAT back, but charges the shop VAT on the product he makes. The shop claims the VAT back, but then charges VAT on top of the price to the customer and the buck stops there. The VAT goes straight to the Customs & Excise via the shop.

The conclusion is obvious – if you're paying VAT on products, goods or services in connection with your self-employment, you should consider applying for VAT registration even if your taxable turnover is never likely to be high enough to make it obligatory. It means that you pass VAT on to your customers and claim back what you've already paid. There are two key words in VAT, *Output* is the sales and services charged out by you and *Input* is all the supplies you buy in, such as petrol, paint, or services. Every three months you have to fill in a form VAT 100, in which you indicate the total tax you've already collected on the sales and services you've provided (output) and you claim back the total tax that you've already paid on your

purchases (input). If you find you've collected more than you've paid, a cheque for the balance must be forwarded to the VAT office at the same time as the return form. If you've already paid more than you've collected you should claim the difference back. This form has to be sent, not to your local office, but to the VAT Central Unit at Alexandra House, 21, Victoria Avenue, Southend-on-Sea, Essex. It's a good thing to photocopy the return form in case of queries afterwards.

You'll have to incorporate a VAT column in your cash book, although you can buy an approved VAT record book from your stationer, which makes it more straightforward to transfer all the information on to the quarterly VAT return form. You must, of course, keep copies of all the invoices you pay, number them and put them in a ring file so they can be cross referenced with the corresponding entries in your cash book. One advantage of VAT to you is that it does actually force you to keep meticulous accounts, which is very important to a self-employed person. I've tried to give you a simplified explanation of VAT and the way it affects people becoming self-employed for the first time. The tax structure itself is very complex, but don't be frightened of it. In any business operation you only have to learn one permutation of the regulations, once you've got this operating VAT becomes routine.

Whilst I've tried to explain the basics of taxes affecting self-employment, it is advisable to get your accounts and tax returns drawn up professionally by an accountant and, if possible, one who knows the peculiarities of your own field, whether you're a musician or a dog-breeder. Most accountants make it a matter of pride that they save you more than they charge, they're experts in 'tax minimisation'. However, you are the one legally responsible for the correct declaration of your profits, so don't try to shelter behind your accountant's professional reputation. Reveal everything honestly to your accountant and the rest will be done for you – *legally*. With tax it's not only a case of presenting your accounts, but there's also consultation with the tax inspector, agreeing just what allowances and adjustments are permissible and the proportion that is taxable. Even if you intend eventually to do your own accounts, get an accountant to do them for the first year or so to establish a pattern of presentation that you can follow later. If the inspector doesn't receive your accounts early enough, you'll be sent an assessment of your income for that year, usually much too high. However, if you don't dispute it, you'll have to pay the full amount and the next year it will be even higher, on the assumption that the first guess was too low. Therefore, it's important that you or your accountant should appeal against the assessment within thirty days of receiving it, and apply for a postponement of the overcharged amount. If the inspector then agrees to your revised figures, you pay that.

Chapter 10

Insuring Yourself

When you're dealing with insurance as a self-employed person, you'll find that there's good news and bad news.

The bad news is that you don't get as much back from the DHSS as you would as an employee. And if you're starting your own business you'll have to look into your existing insurance policies to see if they need modifying, which may mean higher premiums, and you'll probably have to take on new policies that you didn't need before. The good news is that the State allows very generous tax concessions for self-employed people joining private pension schemes, and the other insurance premiums connected with your business are allowed against income tax. Insurance is a pretty boring subject to most of us. But do read this chapter, it might be very important to you and it has been made as simple as possible.

National insurance As soon as you become self-employed, notify your local Social Security office.

As a self-employed person you'll be liable to pay Class 2 contributions until you reach the age of 60 as a woman, or 65 as a man. After that you'll be exempt, even if you do go on earning. The rates change at the start of each new tax year – at the moment they're £3.50 per week. You pay by buying stamps each week from the post office, or by arranging a standing order through your bank account or giro. If you earn less than about £1,950 per year, you should apply to the social security office to be exempted on the grounds of small earnings. But, you'll need to check whether this will affect such things as your retirement pension which you may have accrued previously. You'll also be automatically exempted if you are incapacitated for work. Unfortunately, with Class 2 contributions you're not entitled to claim unemployment benefit as you would if you'd been an employee on Class 1. To claim sickness benefit when you're self-employed you'll need to show some evidence of your normal earnings, and here it would be useful to show your latest tax returns. If you want more information there's a DHSS leaflet NI 41, which you can get from your local social security office. In addition to the weekly Class 2 contributions you'll have to pay a type of tax, called a Class 4 contribution, but you get no benefits from it in return. It's a percentage of your annual profits – currently 6.3% between £4,150 and £13,780. It's collected with your Schedule D income tax at the end of the year by the Inland Revenue. They'll tell you all about it in their leaflet NP 18 from the tax office or social security office.

Home and business insurance   When you start working from home, on however small a scale, you're in theory invalidating your householder's insurance policy. If you have a look at your policy, you'll find you've signed something that says, 'The building is occupied solely by myself and family, and no business is carried on therein'. It will also exclude any liability arising from your trade, profession, business or employment.

Don't think that you can ignore this and do nothing about it, the crunch would come when you tried to make a claim. The company would be entitled to refuse to pay up, because the policy would be invalid, even if the claim had nothing to do with your business activities. For activities such as translating or typing, the company will probably be willing, if you pay a little extra premium, to go on covering the premises as though it were a private dwelling. However, if you have people coming and going from your house on business, this could well affect your cover for third party liability, fire and theft. You must tell the company if you're going to use any part of your home for anything other than a normal residence. The extra cover you'll need will depend on the type of work you're doing at home and the equipment you're using. The company will probably say there are more fire and burglary risks and they may wish to inspect your home so that they can tell you what extra protection you'll need, such as more locks or fire extinguishers. Most business activities won't add much to the fire hazard, unless you're using adhesives or plastic foam which might be regarded as a fire hazard if you're doing upholstery, for example. There are many different kinds of insurance policies and you must ensure your house and business are insured adequately. Below is a list of different insurances which could be useful to you.

Theft and damage to contents It's essential that you insure the contents of your house or business, including the fixtures and fittings; the tools and other equipment; stock, including the supplies you've not yet used; also goods in transit to the customer in your own or someone else's vehicles or sent by post.

Consequential loss insurance This is in addition to the material damage insurance and covers further losses which could occur if your business were to come to a halt. If, for example, your premises burnt down, not only would you need to rebuild and re-equip but your overheads would continue even though there's no money coming in. You may lose all your stock, office records and files and by the time you are back on your feet your customers might have gone elsewhere. This insurance will cover you for loss of profits and overheads for about a year, though you'll probably be able to negotiate for longer.

Employer's liability insurance You must, by law, be covered by this insurance if you employ anybody apart from your own family, domestic servants or independant contractors. It covers any claims you might have if an employee suffered injury or illness resulting from their employment, from a broken wrist to losing a leg. They would, of course, have to prove that it was not their own fault but because of your negligence. It would also be wise to include the members of your family you employ as well, even though it's not absolutely necessary.

Public liability insurance This is an equally essential type of insurance to cover you for claims by members of the public who have been injured or had their property damaged by your negligence. Public liability insurance would take care of the compensation and costs awarded against you, also the costs involved in your defence.

Product liability insurance This covers you for claims arising out of faults in things you have manufactured or serviced. For example, if the vacuum cleaner you've repaired gives someone a severe electric shock. In some occupations this insurance can be difficult to get, especially in new businesses where the insurance company has only your word for it that you'll be conscientious and careful.

There are also things called 'Package Policies' which may, in some cases, be a good deal cheaper than taking out separate policies, but these could involve you in paying for some insurance you don't need and in not getting enough cover for your real risks. Insurance is expensive and you may find that over the years you've paid thousands of pounds out without ever making a claim, but just think; one fire or legal action against you could wipe out years of work if you're not insured. Therefore, you must check each year that items like contents' insurance really represent the current replacement

values, also make sure that you pay your premiums on time – if this is overlooked it's your funeral.

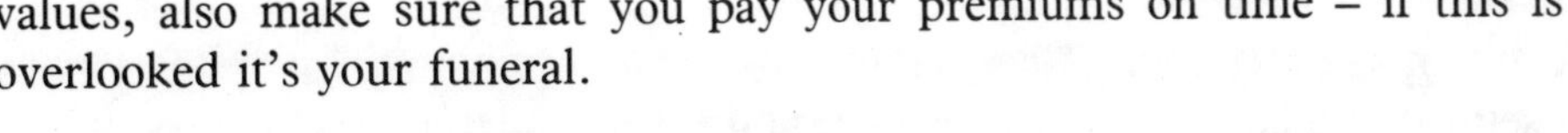

Car insurance   Once you're self-employed do look very carefully into your car insurance policy, which normally excludes commercial travelling. Even if you're just using your car for delivering or collecting orders tell the insurance company. They'll want to know exactly what volume of business you're doing in this way. It may cost more but don't try to hide anything; if you're involved in an accident and they find out that you're carrying goods, and shouldn't be, they would be justified in refusing to pay out. Strictly speaking, if your car is on hire purchase and you're going to change its use, you ought to advise the hire purchase company too. By the way, if your work means a great deal of driving it's only common sense to insure for loss of your driving licence. Through failing the breathalyser, for example, which again might mean the loss of your livelihood. The insurance wouldn't restore your licence, but at least it could supply you with a chauffeur.

Insurance brokers   By the time you read this far, you'll realise what a minefield the insurance business is, so it's a very good idea to employ an insurance broker as it makes life much simpler.

Insurances bought through a broker don't cost you any more either, because brokers are paid by the insurance company in question. You will be advised exactly what insurance you'll need and it will be negotiated for you by getting quotes from different companies. Your broker then collects your premiums, and helps you if and when you need to make a claim. Do make sure beforehand that the person you're considering is a *registered* broker, which should confirm competence and integrity, and not just someone who calls himself an insurance consultant. Some brokers, however, are agents for a limited number of companies, although they probably won't tell you that. Consequently they offer a more restricted service than one who has no links at all.

Personal insurance   As a self-employed person, you're not eligible to receive earnings related benefits. All you're entitled to is the basic pension, which is quite inadequate on its own. So the sooner you start making additional arrangements the better. There's another reason for this; joining a pension scheme is probably the most tax-beneficial saving and investment you can make.

The government will pay at least thirty per cent of your premiums into a private pension fund which itself escapes corporation taxation and the penalties of capital gains. So you would be foolish not to grab at such a bargain. Don't be discouraged from committing yourself to a pension scheme by the thought that your earnings are too erratic and your future too uncertain. Most companies understand the problems of the self-employed and can usually reduce payments if you go through a bad patch and you then catch up later when things improve. There's an awful lot of jargon talked with regard to pensions but they come in three basic forms.

Non-profit – these offer a high guaranteed return short-term, but they won't bring in so much money as a with-profits plan after about five years. This is useful if you're going to retire soon and want a guaranteed income, but if you're under fifty-five forget it.

With-profits – these don't offer such a high return but there's a bonus offered every few years, so it should eventually bring you more money. It's the best bet if you've rather a long time before retirement. On retirement you can choose to have part of your pension paid in a lump sum as well as a reduced pension. The lump sum is tax free up to three times the amount of your pension. You might use this to buy a home or a high income annuity, or even to travel round the world to visit relatives or friends.

Unit-linked – these schemes are inevitably speculative and your premiums are paid into a fund used for professional market investment. You could do badly, but you could also make more money than with a with-profits plan. It's a bit of a gamble. With pension schemes, you'll be bombarded by salesmen competing for your custom. They'll all extol the virtues of their own schemes and knock the opposition, but the best plan is to let your broker make recommendations.

Before suggesting a policy, your broker would need to know from you, when you want to retire and what provision you want to make for your dependants. He would also take into account any existing pension arrangements you may already have, perhaps from a previous employment. It's often better to come up with a mix rather than just one policy, and your broker may suggest that you split your options between a with-profits policy and a unit-linked scheme, thus getting the best of both worlds. You must decide too, whether you want to make regular payments or pay a lump sum every six months or year, possibly because of your irregular earning pattern. You should review these arrangements from time to time, taking into account the current inflation rate plus any changes in your own circumstances.

Private health schemes   Now you come to the controversial topic of private medicine and the taunt of 'queue-jumping' from some sections of society. No one is denying that the NHS provides emergency treatment which is as good as any in the world, but less urgent conditions can lead to long hours in out-patient clinics or months, even years, on a hospital waiting list before being summoned at short notice for an operation. At the moment there are about 700,000 people waiting for 'non-urgent' operations in NHS hospitals.

As a self-employed person I really can't afford this sort of uncertainty. I've only got one body and it seems only common sense to pay to look after it, even if it means going without some of the other luxuries in life. So I've joined the five million people in the UK who've covered themselves by private health insurance – roughly one person in eleven. The largest proportion of these are covered by the three major associations, British United Provident Association (BUPA), Private Patients Plan (PPP) and Western Provident Association (WPA). You'll find their addresses are at the back of this book. It works like this; a privately insured patient is referred by his GP to a specialist in his consulting rooms and if surgical treatment is needed it can be arranged quickly. If the consultant decides that treatment is

not urgent then the time can be arranged to suit the patient. It also means that you can choose your own consultant and know that you'll not be passed on to someone else. You can choose the hospital with the right medical facilities that is most convenient to you. You'll also get privacy, with a single room, a telephone and flexible visiting hours, which allows the convalescent to keep in touch with contacts and perhaps catch up on paper work which is not easy in a public ward. The association then pays all the resulting bills. Another important aspect of private medical insurance is the thorough and regular medical checks, ensuring that any illness detected can be caught in the early stages.

Of course private medicine is not cheap and there is a wide variety of costs depending on age and the specific scheme you prefer. My own costs, which include my wife, come to about £36 a month. As with all insurance there are exclusions, such as routine dental treatment, sight-testing, cosmetic surgery and normal pregnancies. Another provision is that they don't cover any ailment which the patient was suffering from before the policy was taken out. To show you how private health costs can soar alarmingly without health insurance, let me tell you about my son, who recently had a cartilage operation on his knee. Although it was very straightforward and he was in and out in the same day, the total costs of the separate hospital, surgeon and anaesthetist's bills came to £581. He's since decided to join a health scheme himself and pays £11.50 per month, being under thirty.

How to make a will   When I mentioned to my broker that I was about to write a chapter on insurance he said, 'Well, make sure you tell them about making a will – it's one of the most important things of all.' It's all too easy to shy away from making a will but it really is very important. If you happen to die without making one, your family could find that they have an awkward and expensive situation to deal with.

Obviously the safest and easiest way to make a will is to go to a solicitor, who will charge you about £20 upwards. But if your affairs are very simple and straightforward there's no reason why you shouldn't handle the whole matter yourself. You can buy a will form from any good stationer and it will have detailed instructions and examples included to help you fill it out. Your signature must be witnessed by two people who both sign in your presence and in front of each other. They mustn't, however, be relatives or anyone who benefits from the will itself. You'll also need an executor, or better still, two, to handle the terms of the will, but make sure first, that they agree to take on the responsibility. If you prefer you can appoint your bank as executor. Always refer to people by their proper, full names and preferably state their relationship to you. Make sure you clearly state the articles, other than money, to whomever you wish to bequeath. If, in the future, you change your mind, it's much better to destroy the old will and start afresh, though it's possible to make alterations called a 'codicil'. It's important to remember that if you remarry, your existing will automatically becomes invalid so you'll need to make a new one. If, however, you're leaving any major assets or estate, such as securities or properties, it's better to consult a solicitor as he'll probably be able to save your dependants a lot of taxes.

Chapter 11

Coping with the

You may find that when you try to start a new business on your own, you get the distinct impression that one half of officialdom is busy encouraging you to have a go, and the other half seems to be doing its utmost to prevent you. To become your own boss you don't need a licence. Having said that, however, you won't get far in self-employment before you run into some regulation, licence or law.

Change of use and planning permission The first hurdle that you're liable to encounter when you're starting on your own, is the 'Planners'. In theory you're supposed to get permission from the planning department of your local authority to use even part of your house for any income earning activity. But most planning officers turn a blind eye to it as long as it's on a very small scale. However, having said that, it's better to be safe than sorry.

Law

The whole thing revolves around the phrase, change of use. Strictly speaking you need planning permission to use your garage to store goods, to sell things from your house or even to use one room as a work room or office. Whether this permission is granted, or even required, depends to some extent on the sort of activity, whether you employ anyone else or whether the business is likely to affect your neighbours. For example, if you decide to use part of your living room to do freelance commercial art you probably won't need consent for change of use, as the house would still remain basically residential, and it won't create any nuisance to your neighbours. Indeed, unless you say anything no one would even know about it. However, if you have a private house in town and you decide to put a machine in your front room to repair shoes and leave your front door open to customers, then you will certainly need consent for a change of use from residential to commercial. The planning committee would have to consider it, after giving your neighbours a chance to object. Taking things a stage further, if you intend to build an extra room, or convert a garage or put up an out-building, it's vital that you apply first for planning permission. Otherwise when the authorities find out, they can issue an enforcement order to restore the property to its former state. The fact that planning permission would probably have been granted anyway, if you'd applied for it, may not count. Local authorities tend to throw the book at offenders. Even if you make a 'change of use' of the property without seeking consent, the authorities can get tough about that too. They have the power to issue a 'stop order', bringing your business to a grinding halt. If this isn't obeyed within four days you are liable for a fine, so it's just as well to make friends with the folks at the town hall.

However, you can get an enormous amount of help when tackling these procedures by employing the services of local architectural consultants. They are not qualified architects, but are specialists in dealing with local authorities and seem to be on first name terms with the various planning officers because of their day to day contact. They seem to know exactly what they can get away with and what they can't. They also know how to meet the requirements of the building regulations as well. Some of them are so confident of this that if they accept a job, they do it on a no planning permission, no fee basis. There's a fee, at present of £44, payable to the local authority when you apply for planning permission for a 'change of use'.

If, in the end, the planners do turn you down, you can still send off an appeal against their decision to the Department of the Environment which weighs up the evidence from both parties and inspects the site before finally pronouncing judgement. Planning permission for new building work may be given in two stages. First you apply for 'outline planning permission'. If the planning committee agree, it means that in principle, they've given you the green light to go ahead with the expense of preparing and submitting detailed drawings and architects' plans for final planning permission. That's why you often get properties offered for sale saying 'outline planning permission obtained'. If and when you do get planning permission, the planning department, through a gentleman's agreement, informs the rating authority, which pass it on to the valuation officer, who will then probably come to inspect your house about reassessing the rateable value of the part you are now using for your business. The rate in the pound may then go up on that part from the lower domestic tariff to the commercial tariff.

Covenants, leases and building societies   Another thing to check on when you're starting a business at home is that you're not breaking any covenant in force on your house, whether it's rented or bought, so look into the lease or the deeds, first. It is quite possible that a restriction may have been imposed when the estate was originally built, or your landlord might have put a restrictive covenant in the lease. However, they're not all strictly enforceable and you can often get out of them with the help of a solicitor.

If you're buying your house through a building society, make sure that there's no objection to your new business activity. Probably when the house was originally mortgaged, it was done solely as a family residence. However, most societies are quite reasonable and as long as any necessary planning permission is obtained and any possible covenant complied with, they're usually quite happy.

Separate business premises   If you decide not to work at home and buy separate business premises instead, make sure that you check first on existing planning use. If you want a different use, make absolutely sure that you can get permission before you put your money down. For instance, if you buy a shop it can be used for normal retail trading, but you will need further permission if you want to open it as a café, restaurant or pet shop, and you'll also have to get a special licence if you want to venture into the exotic area of sex shops, coffee shops or amusement arcades. Again, if you thought you'd found an empty shop as an ideal site to manufacture washers, you'd have no chance at all of getting 'change of use' unless the area had already been zoned for light industry.

Also, you are entitled to security of tenure, just as if you were the tenant of a private house, if you rent your business premises. You can't be evicted without a good reason and without the proper procedure being followed, often entitling the tenant to compensation. Don't sign any agreement without first having your solicitor inspect the small print or you may find yourself deprived of this protection. A few pounds spent on a solicitor at this stage, might save thousands later on.

Licences and registration   Many trades and professions have to be licensed by the local authorities. Fortunately, most of these procedures are no more than formal registration and, to be fair, are in the interest of the public. Furthermore, one is rarely concerned with more than one item concerning his or her particular trade. Just to give you an idea, they cover such diverse subjects as pet shops, caravan sites, riding schools, ice-cream makers, nursing homes, porters, snack-bars, performing animals and money lenders. If you're a publican you come off worst of all with an absolute maze of regulations. If you buy an existing business, your solicitor will deal with all this automatically. If you're starting from scratch, then the best thing is to ask your local authority if your job needs registering.

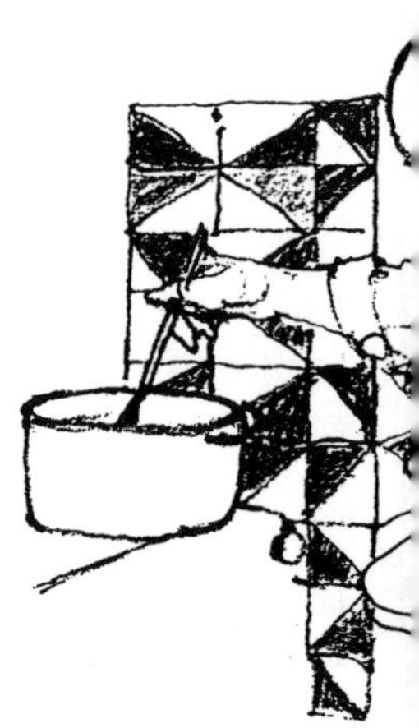

Fire certificates   If you use your home for bed & breakfast, you're all right if you sleep up to six people including staff. However if you offer more accommodation, or anyone sleeps below ground level or above the first floor, you need a fire certificate. The fire prevention officer will come from the local fire authority and inspect your home and tell you what alterations are necessary. These may be fire resistant smoke doors, a fire alarm system and various fire extinguishers. You'll also be given a time limit for the work.

Staff regulations   When you advertise for, or interview prospective staff, remember that the job must be open to all races and both sexes but if you employ less than six people you're usually exempt from the sex bit but not the race. If anyone works for you for more than sixteen hours a week you must provide a contract of employment within thirteen weeks of their commencing work. Also you must deduct tax and be responsible for paying both your own and your employees contributions to National Insurance – their contributions, of course, are deducted from their wages. Outworkers are usually classed as casual workers and are responsible for their own tax and National Insurance.

Preparing food for the public   If you prepare food at home for sale, you come under the Food Hygiene Regulations so contact your local area environmental health officer for advice before you start business. Your premises will then be inspected and here are a few of the things he'll be looking for: easy to clean walls and working surfaces. Any lavatory used by people preparing food must have an adjoining wash basin which must not be used for cleaning equipment or food preparation. No animals should be allowed in the kitchen, and no food should be allowed to stand on or near the floor. Cooked and uncooked meats must be kept separate. A good thing to have is a publication called *Your Guide to Food Hygiene* which is available from the Health Education Council.

Rooms to let   Before you let rooms in your home, first check with your building society if you have a mortgage, or your local housing department if you live in council property.

To find out the amount of rent to charge, you can visit your local rent assessment panel office and ask to look at their Registry of Reasonable Rents. However, if you're thinking of applying to the local university for student tenants, they'll probably advise you what to charge. You should take a returnable deposit against possible damage or moonlight flits, but this shouldn't be more than two months' rent. If you want to get rid of your tenant and the letting isn't for any set period, you must give at least four weeks' notice. If, however, the tenant refuses to leave you can get a court order from the county court, which is obliged to grant you possession, but may postpone the order for up to three months. Please don't take the law into your own hands and try to evict your tenant without a court order, or withhold gas or electricity or by bullying, because this, I'm afraid, is a criminal offence. If you want more information, you can get a free leaflet from your local council office called 'Letting Rooms in your Home', published by the Department of the Environment.

Chapter 12

Learn from the W and the Losers

With every activity you take up, it helps enormously to have an inspirational figure before you to emulate – to give you that shot of adrenalin when you're struggling, and to provide an incentive for the hours of hard work. Sport has its own star figures, the cool dignity of Steve Davis in snooker, the absolute commitment of Boris Becker in tennis and the swash-buckling performances of Ian Botham in cricket. This applies particularly if you're going into business on your own, partly to drive you on but mainly so that you can borrow a star's philosophy and logical approach, and perhaps, adapt it to your own circumstances, however lowly. Here are five examples of my own, which without doubt have encouraged me.

Audrey and I are essentially a husband and wife team, and over the years we've held Laura and Bernard Ashley in almost reverence. When Laura died, it had almost the same impact on me as President Kennedy's assassination. Theirs had been one of the most successful business partnerships since the war and was based firmly on the soundness of their marriage. Like many happy couples, they were opposites in many ways. He had the energy and business sense and was the driving force, while she was the inspiration and the flair. The secret was the way in which their individual talents were interlocked as a team. She was born into a working class family in South Wales and he was the son of a Brixton grocer who, at one time, had been a barrow boy. They were married soon after the war and began their business in 1953. Today, it's an international company with over 200 shops, employing more than 4,000 people and with a turnover of over £100 million. When the company went public just after her tragic accident, the rush for the shares was incredible. These are the bare facts but it's the human story behind it all that has so much to teach the would-be business man or woman.

Going back to the beginning, while Laura was working as a filing clerk at the Women's Institute she attended an LCC printing course and her husband was studying at evening class for his accounting exams. The first 'Ashley' product was a white handkerchief decorated with black noughts and crosses which they sold to Harrods; these were followed by tea-towels, all printed in their kitchen. One of the reasons for their success is the strong individual image she created, filling a part of the market that no one else had touched, the world of the Edwardian lady, the atmosphere of a Georgian

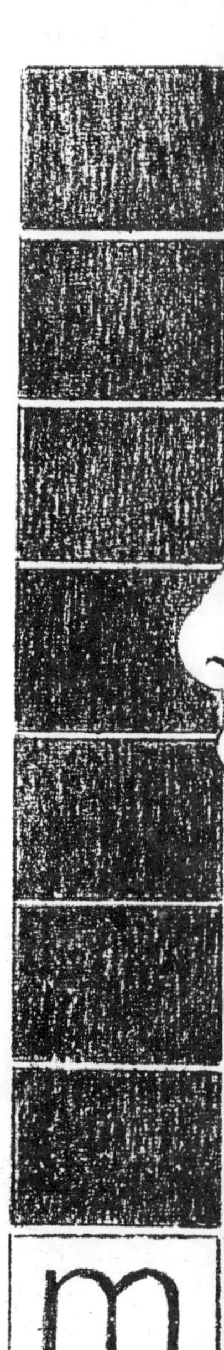

nners

country house, while everyone else was producing bright, brash clothing. She offered a complete life-style, a total concept, a country garden view of life which was sharply defined, recognisable and unchanging. She moved into clothes, furnishing fabrics, wallpaper, and even paint. Laura, as a character, was a good woman in every sense, who believed that work was a moral imperative and was very impatient with people who didn't use their talents and energy continuously. She had many Victorian values, so often scoffed at today when many folk think that hard work is a dirty word. Success didn't spoil them as a family unit either. Although they had their own private jet in which to visit their ever-growing world network of shops and owned a house in St. Tropez, their real home was the farmhouse in Wales where their children grew up and where they started their business.

My next source of inspiration is Sir Terence Conran, very much a contemporary of the Ashleys, who did for the new what they did for the old. When he left art school in the 1950s he had idealistic views on furniture design, but ran up against the brick wall of the traditionalists of the trade who claimed his designs would never sell and that they knew what the public wanted. Basically, it was this frustration of the blinkered complacency that provided the initial driving force. In fact his whole career seems to have been a process of proving 'them' wrong.

He formed a chain of 'Habitat' shops as an outlet to sell his ideas. The shops were equally as individual as Laura Ashley, although in complete contrast. Habitat had a strong overall image which catered mainly for the young. It worked and prospered – yet Conran still had his doubters. The banks refused him when he wanted to expand into America, considering him too 'trendy', so he had to go to Holland to be taken seriously and to be given the capital he needed. Since then his success has been continuous, his influence has increased and he has taken over such companies as Heal's, Mothercare and British Home Stores.

Though a wealthy man now he still has enormous energy, drive and a zeal for design – constantly putting his early sound ideas and attitudes into larger and larger projects and seeing them work. He wants to show how good design can make life more pleasant and in the process provide people with jobs. The inspiration for this punishing schedule is a need to demonstrate that there is a better way of doing things.

One of his complaints is that Britain seems to distrust success. 'If you're struggling and losing money – you're a hero, but if you're struggling and making money – you're regarded as a bloated capitalist.'

I've watched with great interest and fascination the mixture of flair and

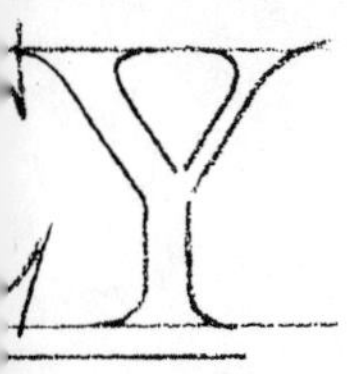

downright common sense he uses to put new life into tired, complacent and ailing companies.

Another source of inspiration to me is a completely different character. He's young and unconventional but uses the same magical mixture – his name is Richard Branson. He left Stowe School at sixteen and started a magazine called *Student* by using a combination of young audacity and imagination, which has since become his driving force. He later opened a small mail order record business over a shoe shop in Oxford Street – the rest is history.

Only twelve short years later his group is worth £200 million and the record company 'Virgin' is one of the biggest in this country.

He's diversified into many other areas: videos, cable television, recording studios, night clubs, real estate and finally his own airline – and he's still only in his early thirties. From his houseboat offices on London's Regent Canal he runs his empire with a £400 million turnover.

His big breakthrough came in 1973 when he signed an unknown musician called Mike Oldfield for his embryo record company. Oldfield's first record sold over seven million copies, giving Branson the capital to branch out into other areas.

He is constantly thinking of new ideas, and says he learnt early on that there are still hundreds of things waiting to be done. He's achieved an enormous reputation for generosity towards his employees and industrial disputes are so far unheard of. He feels that if his staff thought it necessary to be protected by a union, he'd want to know what he'd done wrong to warrant it.

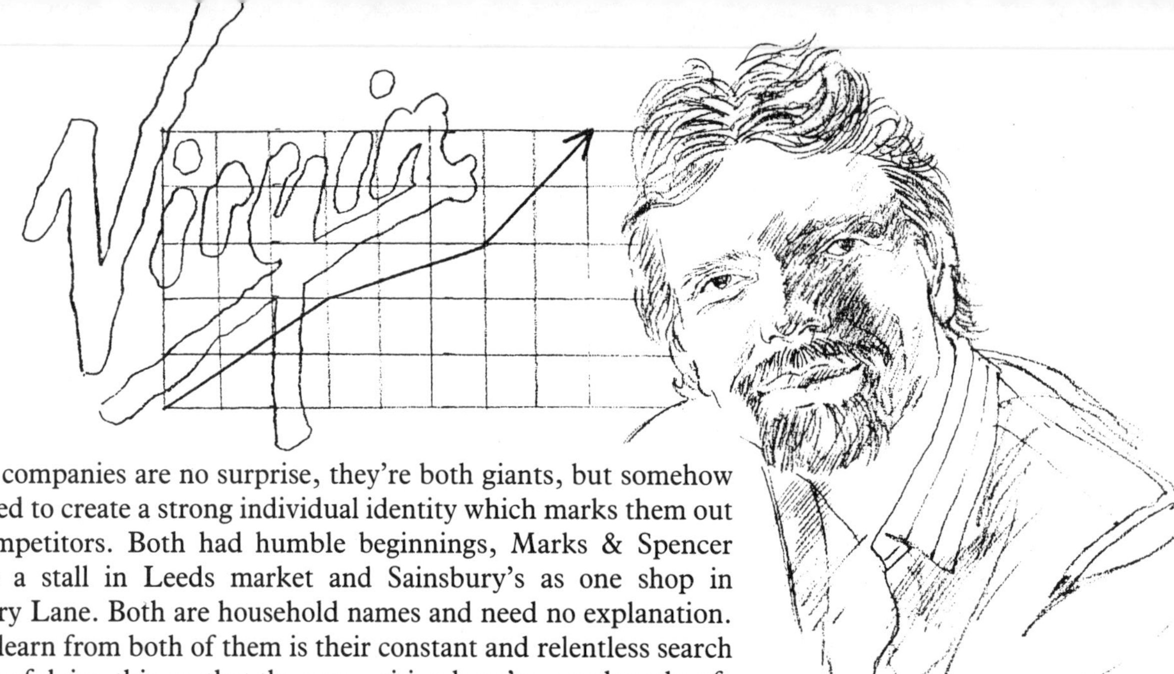

My last two companies are no surprise, they're both giants, but somehow they've managed to create a strong individual identity which marks them out from their competitors. Both had humble beginnings, Marks & Spencer started out as a stall in Leeds market and Sainsbury's as one shop in London's Drury Lane. Both are household names and need no explanation. What you can learn from both of them is their constant and relentless search for better ways of doing things, that the competition hasn't even thought of.

Marks & Spencer's obsession with quality control and value for money has given them a world wide reputation. They give their suppliers a hard time, even minutely inspecting their premises before taking them on – but this has paid off. Constantly questioning accepted practices and delving into new fields, they use the same critical standards whether it's sausage rolls, indoor plants or sweaters.

Sainsbury's have managed to keep the family business intact and constantly growing through four generations. Perhaps this is why they've been able to retain such a strong identity. They're even into DIY, and this strong individual management direction is evident here too. The atmosphere in their new shops is different from any similar establishment.

There are lessons also to be learnt from companies which have recovered their image and pride from the brink of disaster. For example, a few years ago Jaguar cars nearly lost everything due to a disenchanted work-force, weak management, and poor sub-contractors. Their reputation suffered especially in their main market, America, where their unreliability gave them a bad name and sales slumped. In the nick of time a dynamic new managing director took the company by the scruff of its neck and revitalised it, made its sub-contractors quality conscious and gave the work-force a new pride in their product. They regained the company's reputation and sales are now booming in the States. There's also a lesson to be learned from Freddie Laker, a man with enormous charisma, personality and drive, who built up his airline with skill and panache. Perhaps his big mistake was to thumb his nose at the opposition, and undercut his competitors by so much that their only solution was to gang up on him, and this they did very successfully. One can almost transfer the same scenario to the high street. A cautionary tale I've always remembered, is that, if you meet a tiger head-on in the forest, always give him the chance to get out of the situation with dignity, otherwise he must attack you or lose face. This same situation can apply whether we're talking about people, companies, unions or countries. The other lesson is to never overreach yourself, you can't have constant growth without consolidation.

After talking about the 'super-stars', I'm going to the other end of the scale to introduce you to a few of my friends, none of whom is likely to have a private jet, but in terms of fulfilment is probably as content as the Conrans and Ashleys of this world. I'm very conscious of the fact that I may be accused of painting too rosy a picture of small scale self-employment. But the one common factor amongst these people is that they're all 'hard grafters', they're not afraid of hard work and long hours in order to get what they want. Saturdays and Sundays are also working days to them.

Patrick and Ann Mills
Below: Their four-page leaflet

Patrick and Ann Mills   When I first met Patrick and Ann in a local pub, they were trying to console themselves over the shock of Pat's redundancy as a lecturer because of government cut-backs. Having discussed various ideas for alternative employment they finally decided on something they could do together, bed and breakfast, and evening meals.

They live in a tiny 300 year old cottage at the end of a country lane, so obviously they weren't going to get any 'passing' trade. I advised them to advertise in *The Lady*, which has just the sort of readership they wanted, and I also designed a simple four-page leaflet for them, producing it with the aid of a local freelance photographer, to follow up the enquiries they received. Whilst this was happening my part time secretary had to leave because of her husband's change of job, Ann took over that too. Another idea occurred to me, my painting courses were always over-subscribed and we decided to use Brook Cottage as an overflow, instead of turning people away. After two years I'm about to lose Ann as my secretary, thanks to the advertising, the leaflets and my students, several of whom are now her confirmed customers. She's full up for most of the year and can't spare the time for secretarial work. Meanwhile, Pat is busy doing things like extending the car-parking facilities and putting wash-basins in the bedrooms.

Bill Spratt Bill was a lorry driver in a local quarry until he was made redundant at fifty. His future looked grim, and he had apparently few skills apart from being practical and good with his hands. We first met when he offered to clean my windows and I gave him a few odd jobs to do. However, I soon realised his true potential. He would tackle anything with energy and enthusiasm that would put a man half his age to shame. Stone-walling, carpentry, gardening, decorating, roofing – it was all the same to him.

His reputation soon spread around the district – you now have to book him weeks ahead. His largest job was to spend about six months completely renovating a large country house, which must have doubled its value for the owner. He's become a respected and sought after member of the community and walks tall when he's not driving his new car. His secret is that he pulls out all the stops, giving tremendous value for money and taking pride in his work.

Bill Spratt

Albert and Dorothy Smith Albert was an area sales manager for a food firm and his wife Dorothy was a music teacher. Both had 'music in their blood' and played in local orchestras. When Albert was fifty, they took a chance and bought a music shop that had been badly run in the previous ten years and was about to close down. They managed to raise the cash for the lease and the small existing stock and then closed the place down for two weeks while they made it presentable. The idea was that Dorothy would run the shop while Albert kept on with his job, so they could still eat. The day they opened they took £8 and Dorothy went home and wept. At the end of the week they'd taken £60. However, at the end of four months they were taking over £1,000 per week, and they began to build up their stock of brass, woodwind and stringed instruments, and also sold classical records, tapes and sheet music. This last department was so successful that they managed to build up a vast stock, enabling them to begin a mail order service.

Two years after starting the venture they felt financially secure enough for Albert to give up his job and go into the business full time, though he'd been giving every spare minute, anyway, to improve the business. This move proved timely, because about nine months later the firm he'd been working for folded, so he would have lost his job anyway. The business was expanding phenomenally and they were becoming known for running one of the most efficient music shops in the country. Their mail order service was by then world-wide and their staff grew to five full-time assistants. Their climax came when they were invited by the Music Publishers Association to attend the annual luncheon in Park Lane, which had some 700 guests from all fields of the music trade and profession. Albert and Dorothy felt rather out of place among all the BBC producers, disc jockeys and pop stars, and were wondering why they were there at all. All became clear when they were presented with the Certificate of Honour for their services to the music trade. It was the first time that the retail trade had been so honoured. This proved a dramatic conclusion to fifteen successful years in music retailing.

Above: The Music Centre

Brian Banfield and Brian Frost
Below: The old working
men's institute with its vast
interior

Beavers Brian Frost was a civil servant living with his wife in a caravan in an orchard, while Brian Banfield trained as a butcher and then got a job in a brickworks.

However, twelve years ago they were working together in a small workshop producing bespoke staircases and windows, but things were shaky with many cash flow problems. Because of that, they decided to change course somewhat and go into picture framing. The turnover was quicker and people seemed to be more willing to spend money on decorative things like frames, than on staircases – frames were also easier to make. Within three years they had outgrown their small workshop and were looking round for bigger premises. An old working men's institute proved to be the answer. It was going cheaply and had enormous amounts of space. They expanded rapidly, and now have three full time workers and up to ten part time employees. Recently they branched out into art materials and a new project – point of sale assembly. Brian Frost left his caravan and bought a big nine-bedroomed house, very reasonably because no one else wanted it, where his wife now runs a thriving bed and breakfast enterprise. Meanwhile Brian Banfield is also teaching woodwork at a local juvenile offenders' institution in the evenings. This is a good example of being flexible enough to change course when things aren't going too well. Also, the men weren't afraid to diversify into other things when the opportunities came along.

Jenny Kennish Jenny's childhood was spent in her own escapist world of wild flowers, animals and butterflies. Her father was a science teacher and she convinced herself that teaching was her vocation. She was married as soon as she left teacher training college and after raising a son and daughter to school age, returned to part time teaching.

Sadly, after thirteen years of marriage came divorce and she was given custody of the children. Faced with financial difficulties, she had to find a full time teaching job. Dying to succeed in something creative, which would give her mental satisfaction, she happened to visit a craft fair and was immediately stimulated by the atmosphere. She had an idea, and went home and turned out boxes of driftwood, dried flowers and books on butterflies and animals. Could she create them in porcelain? She bought some porcelain clay and practised after the school books had been marked and her children were in bed, and soon afterwards bought a kiln. Eventually, after months of trial and some disastrous mistakes she produced her first primroses. For three years she taught during the day and created the sculptures in the evening. She began selling and exhibiting – then came the day when she felt she could support her family and mortgage by her sculpting, so she became self-employed. She is now exhibiting in the big London galleries and she is a member of the Royal Society of Miniature Painters, the Society of Women Artists and the Society of Botanical Artists. She still never knows how much she is going to earn throughout the year, but is managing to finance her son through university and her daughter in sixth-form college. Both have excelled in their exams, despite the trauma of being part of a single parent family. Jenny told me, 'What I do know is that I enjoy every day. I wake up each morning, looking forward to going to work.'

There are probably two lessons to be learned here; one, Jenny developed her lifelong interest in flowers and small creatures and used it as her inspiration. And she also used her sad divorce and the need to rebuild her life as a 'launching-pad'.

Jenny Kennish
Left: Some examples of her exquisite sculpture

You must take great note too of the losers all around you and the reasons for their failure. Being near a small market town, I'm constantly seeing shops open and close again within six months. I have a 'gut' feeling about their chances of survival, which nearly always turns out to be right. Their main trouble is that they seem to completely neglect a market survey before committing their life savings to a new venture. They open a shop or café, seemingly oblivious of the fact that there are already three established businesses nearby doing exactly the same thing. In other words they hadn't established a real need. I even watched someone spend over £250,000 converting an old chapel into a night club not realising that that particular town wasn't sophisticated enough to support it – he's now desperately trying to sell it.

The keywords for success seem to be *product, price, place* and *time.* It must be the right product, and the word product includes a service. It must be sold at the right price in the right place at the right time. In the case of the night club, the product was wrong, and so was the place – and it failed. Another basic ingredient for success is health and the next two chapters are aimed at living a healthy life and looking after your natural 'assets'.

Being self-employed, I believe, brings with it a promise of a longer life. You avoid that psychological barrier of retirement, when so many people seem to drop dead six months after they've left work, partly I'm sure because they think they're no longer useful.

However, as you get older you need to spend more time on 'body maintenance'. When you're self-employed it's even more important to keep your body working on all cylinders than it is as an employee. After all, you can't just take to your bed and send a sick note to the management with the confidence that the monthly salary cheque won't suffer too much. When you're your own boss, and you stop work – the money stops coming in too.

Obviously, I'm not a great authority on health but what I'm trying to do in this section is to give you some commmonsense information about your body and how to take care of it. There's also a further reading list at the back and the books listed are intended to offer more professional advice on each area mentioned. Remember – it's the only body you have!

Fair wear and tear As we approach midlife (which sounds much better than middle age); we have to accept a certain amount of ageing of our components. Rather like a used car, we need to spend more time and care on servicing and give more attention to potential trouble spots before they even begin to fail. If this is done positively with knowledge, there is no reason why you shouldn't reach old age like a vintage car, becoming universally admired and respected by people of all ages. The secret is in that care and attention.

One positive thing you must do at this time of life is to treat yourself to a comprehensive health screening. This is a very thorough analysis of every component and function of your body. It tests heart and lungs, analyses the blood for fat content, and for possible liver, kidney and metabolic diseases, and the urine for possible diabetes. It will not only detect potential disease or disorder in its infancy but will give you an all round picture of your general health. The results will hopefully be reassuring but will probably show ways in which you can improve your health by drinking less, sticking to a better diet, doing more exercise or most importantly, by cutting out smoking. Taking more interest in your health is not the first stage in becoming a hypochondriac – its just plain common sense. Let's look at some of the bits of your body one by one.

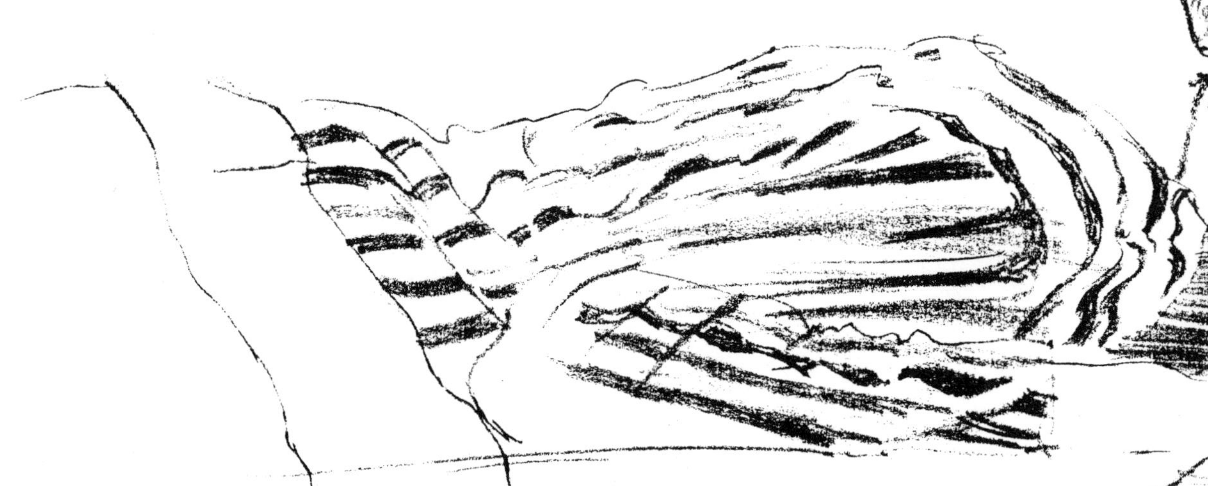

Chapter 13
Body Maintenance

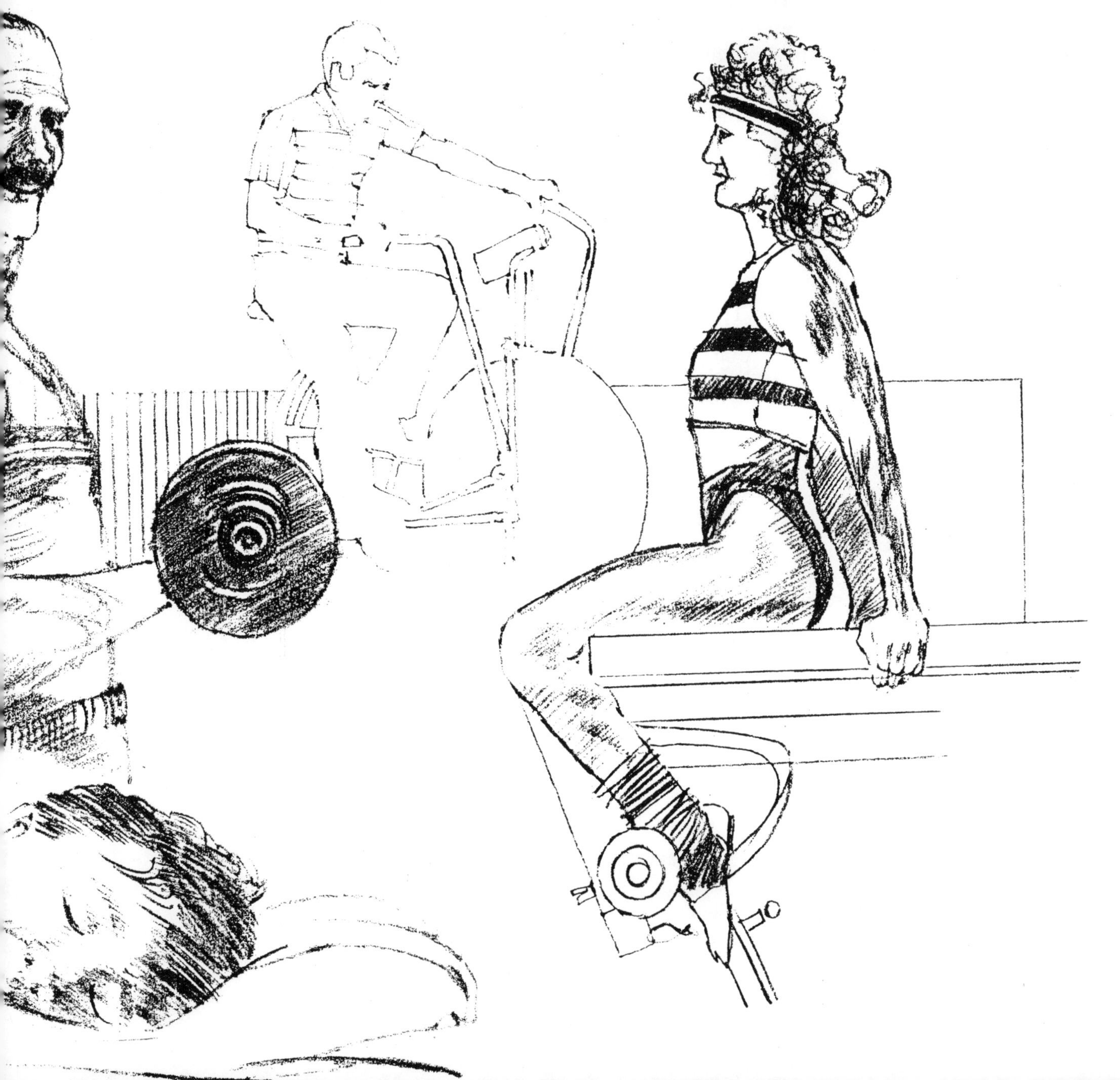

Your teeth   It's not really your teeth you have to worry about in middle age, it's the gums that hold them. In your youth the main trouble is tooth decay, but later this seems to be less of a problem. However, at around forty or so the gums begin to recede little by little which eventually loosens the connections between the tooth and gum until a pocket forms and then the tooth itself loosens. This is by far the main source of tooth loss in middle age, and a further result and perhaps something which is more ageing visually is the loss of the tooth supporting bone itself which can suddenly make your face change from youthful middle age to elderly.

Does that frighten you? It's meant to. The solution is in your own hands. The cause of the whole thing is plaque, a transparent scum made up of millions of bacteria, plus enzymes and food debris. It collects at the base of the tooth, continually attacking the gums and forming tartar, a deposit which irritates the gums and makes a site for more plaque. A normal toothbrush can't shift tartar, only a dentist can remove it by regular scaling and polishing but you can help by thorough brushing at least twice a day. I know you've been told all this before, but most of us find cleaning our teeth such a bore and skimp it and don't do it properly anyway. What you must do is to manipulate the bristles between your teeth into the areas where the plaque collects and then give your gums a scrub in a circular motion and brush upwards and downwards to get the plaque from between the teeth. Other things you can use are interspaced sticks, bought in packets, and dental floss which will help to clean the parts that the brush can't reach. Be careful not to be too vigorous with these though, otherwise you'll find yourself knocking all your fillings out! The whole performance should take no more than three minutes a day, but think of it as a way of preserving your good looks for decades to come. By the way, don't buy a toothbrush that's too hard, the softer ones are more flexible and effective, as well as being kinder to your gums. Change your toothbrush at least every three months because they get tired as well. Of course, you should also visit your dentist every six months for scaling and polishing even if your mouth seems perfectly healthy. When you visit your dentist, always ask to be treated under the NHS otherwise you may be charged as a private patient.

Your ears   As you get older, your sense of hearing becomes less acute too, especially for high-tone sounds. Again this is natural, but it's only sensible to get your hearing checked regularly after the age of fifty, and go straight away if you suspect deterioration.

As you probably know, flying can cause problems with your ears and you often get temporary deafness and even pain due to the sudden changes in cabin pressure. You can help to avoid it during takeoff and landing by swallowing continually or sucking sweets. Another way is to hold your nose and blow, I've seen stewardesses using this method. You'll hear a crackle as the pressure equalises. Try to avoid flying if you have a cold as you'll be more susceptible to ear infection under the low pressure conditions. But if you must fly you could try and use a decongestant spray for an hour or two before and during the flight to avoid pain. Under the circumstances it's advisable

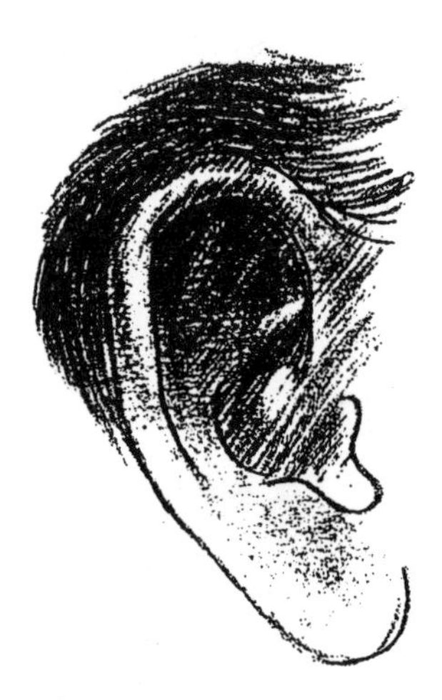

to take the precaution of seeing your doctor first.

Your eyes   One thing you'll notice around the age of fifty, even if you've never had glasses before, is that it seems to get more difficult to read things like 'phone directories and maps at your usual reading distance, especially if it's in poor light. You'll start having to hold things further and further away but don't be scared and think you're gradually going blind. It's really quite a normal ageing process and all that happens is that the lenses in the eyes become a bit less flexible and can't shape themselves to focus tiny details on the retina. The answer is quite simple so don't try to fight it but get your eyes tested free through the NHS at any optician. The glasses prescribed will then have to be paid for but they will give you enormous relief when reading even if you will always be putting them down somewhere and losing them.

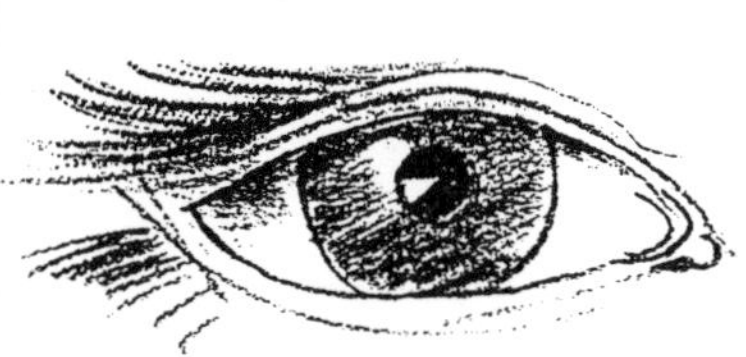

Your eyes may still change a little for a few years so you should get them rechecked annually in case you need new lenses. Other normal changes in the eyes mean that they don't adapt themselves quite so easily to darkness. You actually need about twice the amount of light to do close work when you're in your fifties than you did when you were in your twenties. Avoid overstressing the eye muscles with poor light and make sure that you always have adequate light to work in, if possible, shining from behind over your shoulder for close work. One eye condition which I'm afraid is very common in later years is cataract; this occurs when the lens inside the eye clouds over and the light reaching the retina is gradually reduced. In actual fact most people over sixty-five have some sign of it. Luckily surgery is successful in ninety-five per cent of cases although one usually has to wait for the right stage of the condition before it's operable. Finally, it's common sense to get your eyes tested if you're over forty-five even if you don't think you need glasses. Early detection of a problem pays dividends, and don't forget, it's completely free.

Your feet   Feet are probably the most misused bits of our body. During our youth it's likely that they've been squeezed into badly fitting 'fashionable' shoes and constricted by tight stockings or socks. The fashion shoes of twenty or thirty years ago really were 'cripplers' too – very high heels for girls and winkle-pickers for youths. Things have improved since, and today comfortable, sensible shoes like trainers are 'in'. But for our age group the damage has already been done and this early foot deforming has probably led to corns and bunions in middle age. By this time you've probably also got a bit of stiffening of the joints, so they're not so mobile as before and you may have hammer toes due to the toes being bunched together for years. If you're overweight, too, this obviously puts an even greater load on your feet and can cause local aches and pains.

Having thoroughly depressed you – what can we do about it? The first thing you must do is to make sure that you're choosing the right shoes for the present condition of your feet. Because so many shoe shops are now self-service, you can no longer rely on the assistant's advice and you'll need to use your own judgement, so here are a few tips.

Narrow shoes should be avoided on the whole as, although they may look smart, you'll probably find that you now need a wider fitting for comfort and to avoid pressure.

Try both shoes on as your feet vary in size slightly.

If they have laces, do them up and make sure that the facings don't touch.

Stand up and feel for your longest toe. There should be at least half an inch between the end of your toe and the shoe, if there isn't then get a larger size.

Try to wriggle all your toes freely in the shoe, if you can't, then they're too small.

If, when feeling the widest part of your foot through the shoe, there is a space either side of it, then it's too wide, and if your foot makes the shoe bulge, it's too narrow.

If there's a gap behind the heel when you push your toes up to the front, it's too big over the instep.

Lace-up shoes are best for the feet, as they hold your heel back against the shoe heel, thus leaving your toes more room to move.

Ladies, try to save those high-heeled shoes just for the evenings – in that way they do less harm. Another thing your feet need is a bit of freedom, so try walking round the house or lawn in bare feet when you can. New shoes can cause blisters, so break them in gently and save your well worn shoes for that five mile walk. Don't hesitate to go to a state registered chiropodist. So many people hobble around with painful blisters, corns, ingrowing toe-nails and verrucas when they could get almost immediate relief.

Your back Nearly everyone in middle age seems to have back problems sooner or later, and it's actually now the most common reason for adults to visit their doctor, in Britain. Millions of working days are lost annually through back pain.

The trouble is that our spines were originally intended for walking on all fours and standing and walking upright means that there are lots of stresses and strains on the muscles that link the vertebrae. But it's probably weakness in the abdominal muscles that is the chief cause of our aches and pains. Most of us, myself included, abuse our backs unmercifully. We're inclined to slouch as we get older, hunching our shoulders and letting our stomach muscles get flabby. Being overweight too puts even more strain on the back.

The answer is to concentrate on better posture, but it's difficult to change habits which have developed over the years and you really have to work at it. Try to get someone to tell you when you're stooping (my sons give me hell if they see me). Sit well back in the chair so that it supports your whole weight, and make sure that you don't have to stoop when you're doing your everyday work. If you find that this is happening then change the height of your chair or your working surface. Also, make sure that your mattress is firm enough to support you; remember, you spend at least a third of your life on it. Don't think that its going to last you a lifetime. When it begins to sag, replace it, which will probably be about every ten years. One of the most important things of all though, in preventing back trouble, is learning to lift things properly. You should always flex your knees when you're bending, keeping your back straight and holding your load equally in both hands, close to your body. Nearly all my own back accidents have been caused by neglecting these simple lifting rules. I've no one but myself to blame afterwards for the acute pain and time-consuming treatment. If and when it does strike, painkillers like paracetamol or aspirins help but you may need days of rest to give the muscles time to heal up again. Hot baths and infra-red lamps help too. I've found that going to a registered osteopath once a month for a quick check-up helps enormously, not because there's anything basically wrong but because he can often feel muscle tension building up in a specific area, which he then works on and I come out feeling like a new man.

A final word, do try to walk straight and tall. There is nothing more ageing than a stoop.

Your skin   Don't wash so often as you get older. That may sound a bit drastic, but read on.

Normally the skin is kept soft and flexible by a kind of natural emulsion. The sweat glands secrete liquid, and things called sebaceous glands secrete a kind of grease. This intermixes to lubricate the skin and keep it soft and supple. Adolescents often get too much grease, resulting in spots and acne. Older people though, tend to get too little and the skin begins to dry up. Left to itself the body gets it about right, but we interfere because we've been conditioned into washing too much. Teenagers do need to wash three times a day, but when you reach middle age washing your face with soap and water once a day is probably enough. When you take a bath don't use bath salts or powder as they are also dehydrating to the skin. Moisturising cream is useful for putting back some of the water and grease on the skin.

Sunshine may make you feel good, but it's also ageing. Outdoor workers and people who live in hot climates start wrinkling ten years earlier than those in a dull climate, so if you want a good skin in middle age, stay out of the sun. You don't see many wrinkled nuns even when they're really elderly. I'm afraid that all those magical claims made for the expensive cosmetics are mostly sales talk, and what you're really paying for is the packaging and the perfume. Skin can't be fed from the outside as so many of the advertisements claim, it can only be lubricated. All the moisturisers and skin creams are just emulsions of oil and water which temporarily soften the skin and prevent moisture loss. As well as becoming dryer and less elastic in middle age, the skin often develops patches of pigmentation which may be brown or purplish in colour and are caused by tiny ruptures in blood vessels under the skin. Don't worry, they're quite harmless and are part of the body's normal ageing process.

Your hair   First let's tackle one of the main anxieties of middle-aged men – the thinning and loss of hair. Explaining that it's part of the body's genetic programme and was fixed at birth is not much consolation when you're personally involved. It's no use worrying, there's absolutely no cure for it so don't bother with 'hair clinics' or 'treatment centres'. They just push expensive, scientific sounding massages, lotions, electro-therapy and magic shampoos at you with no real result except that you lose your money as well as your hair. Transplants are another expensive attempt at hair restoring. It doesn't always look much better, and the transplanted hair which is taken from the back and the sides might fall out too.

Baldness is not itself serious, so if you've got it flaunt it. Men like Telly Savalas and Yul Brynner, in my opinion – as a mere man – appear to exude sexual power and neither of them has any hair whatsoever. However, if you must cover up your baldness, a hair piece is probably the answer as long as it's a good one. Again, a bad one fools nobody. Although baldness in women is very rare, a general thinning of the hair is normal as age increases. There are lots of conditioners, sprays and setting lotions which will help to give the hair more body and give it the appearance of being thicker.

Now to the other apparent scourge of middle age – going grey. Though, in actual fact, there's no such thing as grey hair. There's white or unpigmented hair, which mixes with the existing coloured hair to give the appearance of grey. Hair is normally coloured by a pigment called melanin, produced at the base of the hair follicle, which decreases with age. You start with a few hairs becoming unpigmented, and then more and more until the whole head of hair may be white. Again, the original colour and when it goes white are predestined by your father and mother. There are all sorts of rinses, bleaches, shampoos and permanent dyes which can be used to cover up the whiteness, but this is a controversial field in which you have to tread carefully because of possible allergies, and there are even mutterings from various research scientists that some of the chemicals used may be a possible cause of cancer.

Finally, dandruff; this is not a disease, the white flakes are dead skin cells which come off the scalp, but they're more likely to be noticeable when you have greasy hair, so wash it more often. If however you do have a severe case of dandruff get a proper medicated shampoo.

Smoking   Here I feel like the Pope giving advice on birth control – I've never smoked seriously myself. However, I'm determined to give you a few facts about it, even if you have heard it all before.

People who smoke more than twenty cigarettes a day take twice as many days off work each year with sickness as non-smokers, and as a self-employed person you can't afford that. Smoking is also the major cause of illness and premature death in Europe. Apart from lung cancer, which is twenty times more likely to occur in a smoker than a non-smoker, there is also an enormously higher risk of heart disease, bronchitis, ulcers and emphysema – even if you ignore things like yellow teeth and bad breath. However all is not lost, even if you've been smoking for thirty years, it's still not too late. From the moment you stop, you'll look better, smell better, and you'll start resisting disease better and your heart and lungs will work more

efficiently. The risk of cancer becomes less and less until after about 10 years, and then it's no greater than for a non-smoker.

But how do you stop? You've probably already tried once or twice and failed. Forty per cent of British adults smoke, and half of them want to give it up. Unfortunately, half of all the male smokers and a third of the female smokers go on until they die, still coughing. The trouble is that smoking, even if the smokers deny it, is not merely a pleasurable habit but an addiction, and has to be treated as such. There's no easy way of giving it up otherwise more people would succeed. You won't do it unless you have lots of will power. It comes down to motivation. The main task is to convince yourself that smoking is unworthy of you and that it's unhealthy, dirty and expensive. But even that won't work unless you really *want* to give it up. No one can succeed against his will. There are many helpful leaflets published by the NHS for people who seriously want to give up.

You can use all sorts of psychological tricks against yourself of course. Tell everyone around you when you're going to give it up, so that you'll look rather silly if you don't keep to your resolution. Or more morbidly, keep a picture in your mind of someone in bed with lung cancer and frighten yourself. You might also get some friends to sponsor you to stop. Or make a bet with someone that you'll stop for three months. Another way is to make a deal with a fellow smoker to stop together so that you can console and sympathise with one another. In other words publicly commit yourself. Here's yet another method to try. Put off smoking your first cigarette by half an hour each day, but smoke as many as usual after that. After ten days your first cigarette will be at lunch-time and within a month you'll, hopefully, have finished with them completely. Once you've made the break, the main task is to prevent a relapse. Change your routine during the day, if possible, and beware of the danger events, such as cups of coffee, telephone calls, or after meals when you tend to light up without thinking. But if you conquer these moments of intense temptation to smoke you should be well on the way to giving it up altogether. If however, you do lapse, try to find out why it happened and avoid that particular situation in the future. There are more unconventional methods too, which may help you, such as hypnotism, acupuncture and aversion therapy and I've heard very good reports of a product called Nicobreven which may reduce the nicotine withdrawal symptoms.

Be warned, an ex-smoker is just as likely to relapse after a single cigarette as an alcoholic after one drink, so once you've succeeded in kicking the habit, never light up another cigarette, ever. Remember, each cigarette will shorten your life by five and a half minutes. In other words a packet of twenty will mean nearly two hours less living.

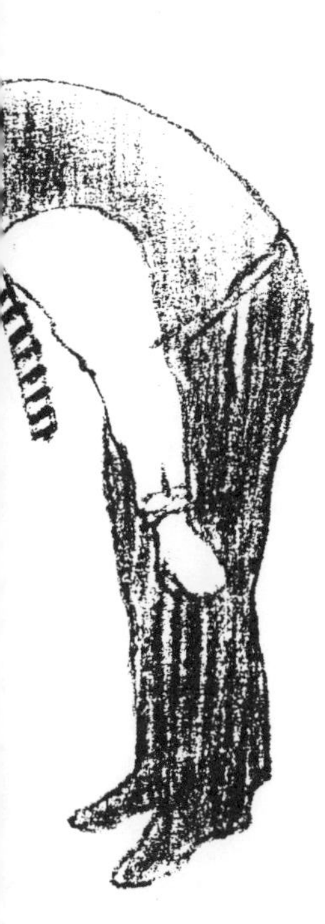

Alcohol 'A drink problem' – this is a euphemistic phrase we all use for alcohol dependence.

Let's be positive about alcohol. Most of us take it in moderation and treat it as a social excuse to meet our friends. In small doses, it relieves tension, gives you a sense of well-being and isn't harmful. Indeed, wine in moderation is known to be good for you. In the main wine-drinking countries of Europe the heart attack rate is the lowest. Having said that, alcohol is really just another drug which makes you feel good, and as such it is potentially addictive. The danger comes when you begin to use it to escape from major problems. Your alcohol tolerance then begins to develop rapidly and you'll find that you need larger and larger doses to achieve the original desired effect. This is when drink ceases to be a pleasure and becomes an addiction. In large doses, alcohol causes chronic depression, misery and self-doubt. Today's alcoholic is not necessarily the meths-swigging drunk in the gutter, which is the usual picture that springs to mind, but could be the well-to-do, middle-aged, educated man or woman who is incapable of doing any useful work in the afternoon. If that person is self-employed as well, then the future is really black.

The whole thing, of course, is on a sliding scale. Most of us are social drinkers – I'm one myself and intend to stay one – but the next stage is the heavy drinker who may develop without realising it into an excessive drinker. This is the point where it becomes a medical problem, and those persons really have to recognise their plight and either cut down or stop their drinking entirely. If they can't or won't, they gradually become alcoholics who drink without control and who can't stop without help. At this stage it not only affects themselves, but can also start to break up marriages and lose jobs, apart from the disastrous long term effects on health. These can include peptic ulcers, cirrhosis of the liver, chronic inflammation of the stomach and brain damage. By the time all these effects have been brought about, the sufferer's personal and professional life has probably already been destroyed. One of the greatest difficulties in preventing the slide down the slippery slope is definitely lack of early recognition of the problem. Potential problem drinkers are hard to identify, especially by themselves. To find out if you yourself are in danger of becoming alcohol dependent, try to answer these questions honestly:

Do you drink alone?
Do you need to have a couple of drinks before you can face a problem?
Is the pub your only social life?
Do you find it impossible to go through a whole day without a drink?
Do you drink for the effect it has on you rather than because you like the taste?

If you answer yes to two or more of these questions then it's time to beware and to take steps to control the situation. Being able to refuse a drink when it's offered to you is a good test too, as there are so many social pressures to drink. It's as well to have a few excuses up your sleeve, so that you can refuse without losing face or causing offence. There's no real need to forgo the social side either, as it may be very precious to you. Just switch to non-alcoholic drinks like barbican, bitter lemon or a Virgin Mary, which is tonic water and lime. Now to drinking and driving; you're certain to be over the breathalyser limit if you have more than the equivalent of three drinks in your system and you may even be betrayed by less. Remember this, there's absolutely no way you can drink and drive safely.

Finally, if after reading all this you believe you may have become addicted, you *must* seek help. Alcoholism is an illness and you should consult your GP and confide in him, or you may prefer contact with one of the organisations listed in the back of this book.

What sort of shape are you in?   Have a good long look at yourself in a full-length mirror and decide if you're proud of what you see or a bit ashamed. From the front, not too bad, *now* stand sideways – stop holding your breath to keep your stomach in. (There's no fooling me, I've done it myself.) I did just that when I started this book and had my photograph taken sideways – I was horrified, so decided to use the book as a way of forcing myself to slim down. I don't know whether I'm going to succeed or not.

The reason for getting fatter in middle age is simple, we tend not to use up so much energy. But we still go on eating at least as much, perhaps even more. So our energy intake is larger than our energy output and the body stores all the rest as fat. Okay, so you're fatter than you should be, but does it matter? Yes it does. Here are some of the reasons. The fatter you are the likelier you are to die early, but if you're fat now and slim down to normal, your chances of living longer go back to normal too. Carrying around extra weight is putting extra strain on your ligaments and joints which probably means more arthritis and back pain. It even means that you'll probably be involved in more accidents in your home or at work, because your greater bulk makes you slower than thin people. First, you must find out your own ideal weight (see the chart below). I'll try to make it as simple as possible,

Below: Weight charts showing ideal weights for men and women

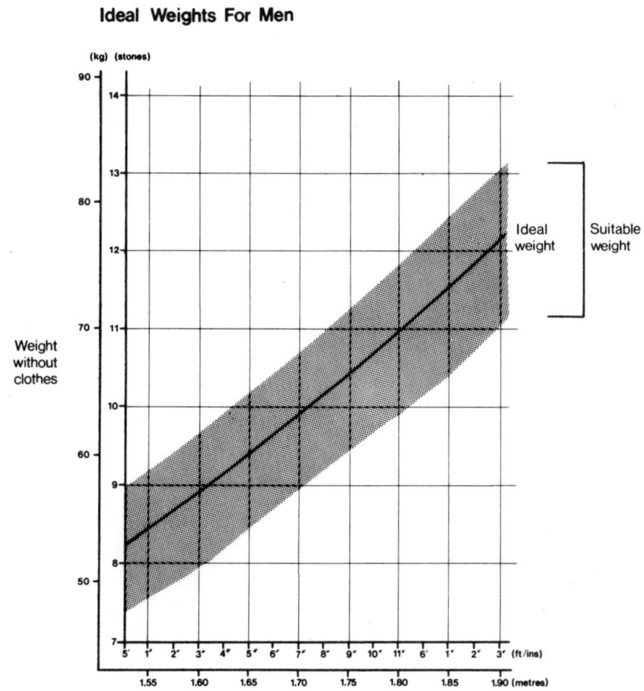

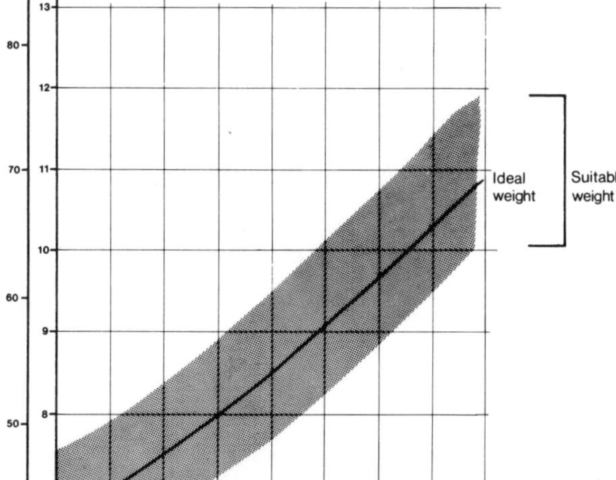

but if you have a calculator handy, it will help. Because a taller person is usually heavier than a short one, height is taken into account in this calculation.

His – W = 21.7 (height in m)^2
First convert your height to m, for example a 6ft man would be 72in × .025 = 1.8m.
His ideal weight would be: 21.7 × 1.8 × 1.8 = 70kg (11st 3lb).

Hers – W = 21.2 × (height in m)^2
Again convert your height to m, for example a 5ft 5in woman would be 65in × .025 = 1.65m.
Her ideal weight would be: 21.2 × 1.65 × 1.65 = 58kg (9st 3lb).

Scientists use a formula which is your weight divided by the square of your height, with your weight in kilograms and height in metres. The ideal result of this should be 21.7 for men and 21.2 for women.

Of course it would be ridiculous to pin-point an ideal weight as exactly this, because people's frame sizes vary, and so do their bones, so it's sensible to allow about half a stone either way. But it's tempting to assume you've got big bones just to kid yourself you're not overweight, so watch it. If your weight falls within the allowed range, forget about slimming. However, if it's at the top of the range or above it – take action. Try to reduce it before it gets any higher. It is advisable though to have a medical check up before going on any kind of stringent slimming regime, especially if you have problems with your health. Let's be completely frank. The only real way to rid yourself of surplus fat is to control your eating and drinking so that your body has to call on its store of fat to supply you with energy. In spite of some of the advertisements you read, there are no magic foods you can eat in order to slim. Fat is only broken down in the body when the output exceeds the energy input.

Now I'll have to bring in that awful word 'calories', which is really just a measurement of energy going in and energy coming out. Every surplus pound of fat on you represents an energy store of 3,500 calories, so to get rid of a pound of fat you must use up 3,500 calories more than you take in. Let's say that you had a 1,000 calories a day 'energy gap' – in a week you'd have lost two pounds of fat. We're always being bombarded by slimming books and fancy diets from every direction. Every film and television star seems to have found the ideal method and is busy making money publicising it. Throughout this maze of fancy diets, there are two basic approaches to dieting which, to me, seem logical and sensible. You'll have to decide for yourself which one will suit your own character best. The first is 'cut-down' diet, in which you count the calories of the various foods, making sure you don't exceed the total intake allowed each day to provide you with your 'energy gap'. It seems to work especially well for women at home, but I don't believe I could keep it up for long, especially the weighing and measuring. However, if you do decide on this method, you can obtain plenty of suitable calorie charts and leaflets about it. (More information at the back of this

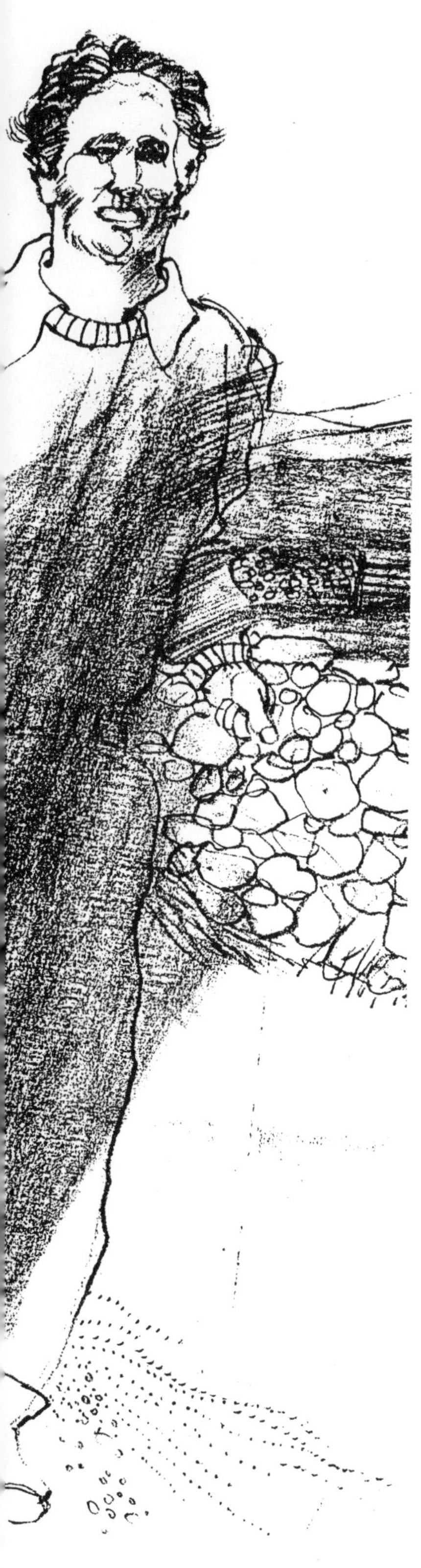

book.) It might seem though, that you'll spend your whole time looking up calories. In fact, because you basically eat the same things every day, you'll soon learn most of it by heart and after a few weeks you'll be able to judge, without weighing, just how much food to put on your plate. The advantage of this scheme is that you can eat anything you fancy so long as you check its calorific value. You can even exceed your limit on one day, as long as you don't exceed your limit over the week. How much energy you expend depends on whether you're a man or a woman, your weight and height and your age. For example, if you're a fairly sedentary, forty-five-year-old woman you can assume you're using 2,200 calories a day, therefore for an energy gap of 1,000 calories you should only consume 1,200 calories per day. If you're a moderately active man of about fifty-five, you'll use 2,900 calories, so for the same energy gap your allowance is 1,900 calories.

The second approach is the 'cut-out' diet, which is the one that seems to appeal to men especially – including me. It's a simple low-carbohydrate plan which basically consists of three lists. The first list is food that you can eat as much as you like, the second list is food with which you must go carefully, consuming only a restricted amount each day, and the third list is food that you must try to cut out completely.

List 1   (As much as you like) – poultry, game, fish, green vegetables, root vegetables (except potatoes), fruit (except bananas), cottage cheese, clear and low-calorie soups, water, black and unsweetened tea and coffee.
List 2   (No more than the following amounts each day) – ½pt of milk, 1oz soft margarine, one egg, 4oz cheese, 4oz meat, 2 slices wholemeal bread, 1 glass of wine or beer, ½pt of soup, 4oz rice, 4oz spaghetti or pasta, 4oz potatoes and 1 banana.
List 3   (Cut these out completely) – sugar, cream, butter, hard margarine, fats and oils, sweets, chocolates, cream cheese, pastry, heavy puddings, syrup, treacle, jam, marmalade, tinned fruit in syrup, dried fruit, crisps, savouries and nuts, salad cream, mayonnaise, rich creamy soups, pies, white bread, breakfast cereals and biscuits.

It's not just a case of knowing the calorific value of each food and having your personal weight target to aim for. The result will probably be that you will fail and put it down to your own lack of will-power. We've got to really look at the reasons why we fail and try to counteract them in advance. Diet has six main enemies: boredom, loneliness, hunger, anger, depression and tiredness. Overweight people who are bored, depressed or lonely tend to use food as a way of combating these moods. Try fighting them off in other ways, such as starting a hobby, joining an evening class or even making a list of things to do when you start to feel hungry. Overeating is often indulged in by people who can't express anger properly, but exercise is a much better way of relieving this tension and also uses up more calories. Tired people often attempt to get more energy by eating more, but it's much better to try to get more sleep or to relax more in the middle of the day. Some of us are more responsive to food stimuli than others. The sight, smell or even reference to food can give some of us an intense desire to eat – this has nothing to do with real hunger at all. One of the things you shouldn't do is to skip breakfast and have a small lunch or you'll feel ravenous in the evening and be tempted to eat a large meal which will more than compensate for all the food you've denied yourself during the day. Evening is always a danger period when our social and emotional needs are strongest and we're most vulnerable to temptation.

How do we keep up the enthusiasm? Slimming is a pretty boring and lonely job, and you need to have lots of intermediate landmarks and encouragement to continue. One idea may be to take part in a sponsored slim. Lots of people will then know how you're getting on, and the more you lose the more that goes to charity. These things usually last from one to two months and by that time you may have lost enough weight to be encouraged to continue. Try slimming with a friend – this should produce a healthy rivalry so that you're constantly checking one another's efforts. It's also important for you to keep an exact visual record of your progress on a wall, as it's very encouraging to see your weight falling on a graph week by week.

Another way of getting support is to join an organisation like Weight Watchers, whose overall aim is to teach members a new attitude towards eating so that they not only lose weight but stay slim for life. There seems to be a branch in most districts. (See in the back of this book for other useful addresses.) Buy a slimming magazine regularly that can act as a morale booster and keep up your interest.

Let's face it – you're bound to have occasional lapses and you'll think you've failed completely, but be constructive about it. Write down the circumstances that led up to it, such as worry, anger or disappointment. Try to identify which are the most vulnerable situations for triggering off your personal eating lapses and plan how you can avoid the situation next time.

Keeping fit We've talked about reducing the calories going in, but by far the best and healthiest way of slimming is to attack the 'energy gap' from both ends at once. So we come to this dreadful business called exercise and keeping fit, and what must now be a new attitude towards your body and diet. With the body, disuse is misuse. It's a very flexible machine and when in good trim, it's capable of an enormous output of energy. Left idle, however, it starts to deteriorate. If you're severely over weight it's advisable to contact your GP about a sensible exercise programme.

If you don't use your muscles (any of them) enough, they begin to lose strength and bulk, and fat starts to accumulate, not only where it shows but around the important bits, such as the heart, intestines and kidneys. I hope this convinces you that you need to take more exercise, but for goodness sake don't go mad at first – start gradually. It's harmful to try and exercise vigorously after a long period of inactivity and I don't want any dead bodies on my conscience. Let's assume you're out of condition at this point, so start by walking, say half an hour a day, walk upstairs instead of taking the lift, do some press-ups in your bedroom or muscle tightening exercises in your car. After a week or two of this you should be fit enough to start some vigorous exercises for a short time each day. These should be energetic enough to start your pulse racing and producing a mild sweat, but do make sure that you're capable of it. If you're an inactive fifty year old, or even younger and overweight, or have a history of heart disease or blood pressure, see your doctor first about any form of exercise.

The danger with all forms of exercise is that after a few days you'll start to lose interest, so you must make plans before you start to avoid this situation. It's much more fun, for example, to exercise with a friend and you can use his enthusiasm to carry you along when you may be getting temporarily disenchanted. Incorporate exercise as a natural part of your life, like cycling to the shops or work, instead of waiting for a bus or going by car. If it's a long way, try walking part of the journey. It may not be sensible to take up a strenuous sport like squash in middle age, although I did just that at fifty-five and thoroughly enjoy it. Probably the most sensible sports are those you can do at your own speed, such as swimming, golf, or cycling. In any case, choose a sport that easily fits in with your present life-style, perhaps where there are good facilities close by for you to enjoy. It may be Scottish dancing for some, or ice skating or badminton for others. From the pure health point of view, you'll gain tremendous benefits from regular exercise – *whether you're overweight or not.*

Chapter 14

Sex in the Middle-ages!

Another facet of an healthy body is a healthy sex life but I think most of us have been thoroughly conned about sex over the years. Books, films and television are constantly bombarding us with ideal love and super sex. You're brainwashed into the idea that everybody else is having a much better sex life than you are. You may read in books by Harold Robbins or Jackie Collins that the hero is making love three or four times a night, or that the heroine has multi-orgasms every time, and you get to the point where you're convinced that you must be some sort of sexual cripple. In other words, you're constantly being presented with images and standards which you have little or no chance of living up to.

It happens in other areas too, of course; just compare your own kitchen with those spotless, hygienic kitchens on the television commercials looking more like operating theatres. However, the idealised kitchen does no harm as you don't believe them and you can always compare your own with the one next door – but with sex it's different. It's not usually done to compare notes on our relative sex lives with our neighbours, or at least it wasn't in our time. The result is that a lot of us feel we're constantly missing out and have a secret inferiority complex about it, made worse because it's bottled up inside us. Another thing that doesn't help is that the younger generation always think they've invented sex and that it's their own personal property. For their own parents to even think of indulging in it at their advanced age is somehow obscene and disgusting, and so, as our children grow up into their twenties and thirties, it becomes a taboo subject and is pushed under the carpet.

The main problem with sex in middle life or even old age isn't the physical side at all, but the shadow cast by misinformed beliefs that sex in later life is not expected and at a certain age one becomes 'past it'. When I was in my forties I though it must be about fifty, and in my fifties I thought that sixty would be the end of it. I'm now told, to my delight, that you can still have a satisfactory love life in your seventies and even eighties. Having written this, I'll probably get an indignant letter from someone in her nineties saying she's been missed out too. The whole thing is in the mind, and these may be misconceptions that many of us have harboured for years but have never seen aired in a book before. Obviously no one's suggesting that your sex drive in your fifties, for example, is as explosive as it was in your teens. But

as with a seasoned veteran on a squash court beating a younger, fitter opponent with super guile, a man or woman's experience and sensitivity to their partner's needs, can probably make them much more satisfying lovers, more than compensating for the energetic power of an eighteen year old.

Now turning to the subject of sexual difficulties. Someone recently did an extensive survey and discovered that possibly sixty per cent of individuals have sexual problems of a significant nature for a substantial part of their lives. This is not meant to depress you, just to show that there's a lot of it about. However, a man who's had problems and anxieties, coping with the stressful periods of puberty and adolescence, marriage and parenthood may find yet another psychologically disturbing period in middle age, coming as it often does, at the same time that his wife is trying to cope with the menopause. Many people who read this book may have lost their jobs recently with all its emotional repercussions. This too, may put enormous pressure on a couple's relationship because of its stressful nature. The re-adjustment itself is wearing, and you may for a period of time become too tense, too tired and too busy for sex. You may become two separate, exhausted people who just happen to live under the same roof and share the same bed.

Male problems   As mentioned previously, sixty per cent of individuals do have sexual difficulties at various times in their lives so now might be a good time to bring them into the open. If you are one of those lucky forty per cent you can skip this bit.

Let's start with the basics. With nearly all sex problems there is absolutely nothing wrong with the plumbing, although it may sometimes seem like it. In fact, it's worry, anxiety and nervous tension which in turn produces an emotion which kills sexual desire stone dead – that emotion is fear. Simply put, in animals the first instinct is self-preservation and the second one is race-preservation or sex. If they mated during danger they would probably be destroyed, so nature has arranged matters so that a dangerous situation produces fear in the male which in turn wipes out the sexual desire completely and he's instantly on his guard. To some extent the same thing happens to the female. This can become a permanent state of affairs and is why some animals won't breed in captivity. We humans have inherited this reaction from our animal ancestors. In some situations we'd all be impotent – if, for instance, someone was pointing a gun at us. Real sexual desire only happens when man is free from fear.

So many folk have their sexual feelings mixed up with feelings of fear that one immediately starts up the other. This is probably because of unfortunate experiences in youth with 'elders and betters' provoking feelings of shame about sex and constantly condemning it as wicked, thus many folk grew up with a fear of their own sexual feelings. In my opinion the church and the chapel have a lot to answer for in this direction with their condemnation of 'the pleasures of the flesh'. When people finally come to marriage they're told it's not sinful any more and it's all right to enjoy it. The trouble is that as the sex desire rises, so do all the ghosts of the past which prevents people from being natural and free, and it's this conflict that seems to account for a huge amount of sexual difficulty.

So we come to middle age and in some cases a few more fears rise to the surface as a man believes he will lose his sexual powers at any moment. At the age of around fifty he may easily become a sexual hypochondriac, complaining of having lost his sexual urge, of premature ejaculation or of recurrent poor erection. This self-obsession may lead to tension, depression, resentment and concern for his male image. During this period some men may try in vain to recapture their youthful appearance and some will even seek out a younger woman who, they hope, will restore their virility and self image.

At this point it is important for a man to realise just what his sexual future is, and to come to terms with it realistically, and not with grudging resentment. It may well be that his sexual prowess and appetite gradually decline as he ages, but this is just a fact of mature sexual life. There will be a gradual lessening of libido, and it may take more time to get an erection and your potential for orgasm may lessen. The physical quality of sex may lessen with age but the emotional pleasure and intimacy should continue to be as great as ever. It's very important during this mid-life transition period that the husband and wife reassure each other of their continued affection and attraction to each other. Otherwise the reduction in sexual activity may make the woman feel that she is no longer desirable and she may suppress her own desires until the man starts to feel rejected too. It all comes down to communication. You'd think that after a man and woman had been married to each other for twenty to thirty years they'd have perfected their communication system. Unfortunately this is often not the case and it leads to misunderstanding and hurt with no real justification. If you have a problem with temporary impotence it's important for a man to understand exactly what is causing the trouble, and the wife's love and understanding are absolutely vital, for the way she handles the situation may make all the difference in the world. A man often feels humiliated when he believes he's failing to satisfy his partner. If she laughs at him, taunts him or is angry and disappointed he will feel utterly crushed. It may even be that his wife's attitude has been the chief cause of his trouble.

Often, because of his fear of humiliation, the man dreads the next occasion and may even try to avoid any sexual intimacy at all. This makes him appear distant and cold to his wife. As a result she then feels hurt and undesired, and the longer this avoidance goes on, the harder it becomes for the couple to attempt love-making again. It's rather like the husband being scared to turn a tap on in case no water comes out, and the wife thinking that he can't be thirsty or even that he's getting a drink somewhere else. In order to put things right, the whole thing must be accepted as a joint task. The woman must be sympathetic and encouraging and not expect him to sort the problem out on his own. It's important to try and change the atmosphere completely. The desire for each other must be brought back into the relationship.

The secret is to make the whole thing a whole lot more lighthearted and less tense. Forget all about complete intercourse and just have fun by caressing each other's bodies for the sheer joy of it. Don't even bother about anything else and in time the whole atmosphere will gradually become free from fear and anxiety. If intercourse is attempted and it fails, the only thing to do is to laugh and say 'Well, better luck next time.' The wife should at all times be encouraging and congratulate any progress, and the confidence this gives him will help enormously. The main thing is to keep the whole process happy and unhurried, until one day, to the couple's surprise and delight, they'll find that all the fears have been shaken off and intercourse is possible. Sometimes it happens this way after years of failure. From the wife's point of view, however, it may be frustrating for her to be continually stimulated to the point of desiring intercourse and then left unsatisfied. This may even be the initial cause of his worries, failing to fulfil his wife. It may be better therefore if he stimulates his wife to orgasm clitorally at the end of the love-play, making the effect as near as possible to actual intercourse. This may not be completely satisfactory but as a temporary measure it may avoid emotional frustration in her and make him less anxious.

Premature ejaculation is another major problem for men and it usually happens when he can't control his ejaculation long enough for his partner to reach her climax. Indeed he may 'go off' before he's made sexual connection at all. Failing and then brooding about it afterwards is obviously the worse thing to do, and like impotence it's a joint operation that needs patience and understanding from both partners to help solve. It may even be that as the woman gets older she takes longer to achieve satisfaction, so the timing becomes difficult. In this case the woman can control things better by being uppermost and doing most of the work. Although it's not such a difficult problem as impotence, the cause and effect are still, usually, emotional and if you can't resolve it soon do get help.

Of course there is plenty of outside help in these matters. The Marriage Guidance Council, for example, runs Sexual Disfunction clinics. But you might say, 'I'd be too embarrassed to go to a sex clinic and talk to a complete stranger about my intimate bedroom secrets'. Okay, it takes courage to make an appointment and probably even more to actually meet counsellors for the first time, but believe me, they do make you feel relaxed so quickly that you'll wonder what all the fuss was about, and just having the chance to talk about things openly can do wonders to relieve the tension. So many of these anxieties arise because we expect too much, and reassurance from an expert will help. Another alternative is sex therapy, which helps people to make love in a more pleasurable way. So, just because you've reached fifty you needn't think you know it all.

Female problems   First, let's be positive and get rid of the myth that your love-life goes off and you become less sexually attractive during and after the menopause. In fact, it can bring positive advantages, and a woman can enjoy new sexual freedom once she's not bothered about pregnancy and she's got her period problems under control. The chances are you'll feel sexier in your forties than you did in your twenties.

'Fine,' you say, 'but will I still be attractive to men as I get older?' At this stage the danger is more in losing your self-confidence, and if you expect to get less attractive then you will be. So much of attractiveness is invisible, like charm, vitality, warmth and a carefree attitude. What *is* ageing is anxiety about your looks, too much make-up and tension. Don't think of yourself as a woman who's perhaps still attractive – you are an attractive woman at all times. In some cases, if you're overweight, slimming can make a difference to your love-life as it will not only make you less worried about cavorting naked but you'll probably feel more agile and sexy. On the other hand, it may be difficult to achieve orgasms. Let's face it, some women never have orgasms at all, and there are plenty of others who don't have them with 'traditional intercourse' alone. In my opinion two of the sexiest and most attractive women are Sophia Loren and Cleo Laine, both well into their fifties.

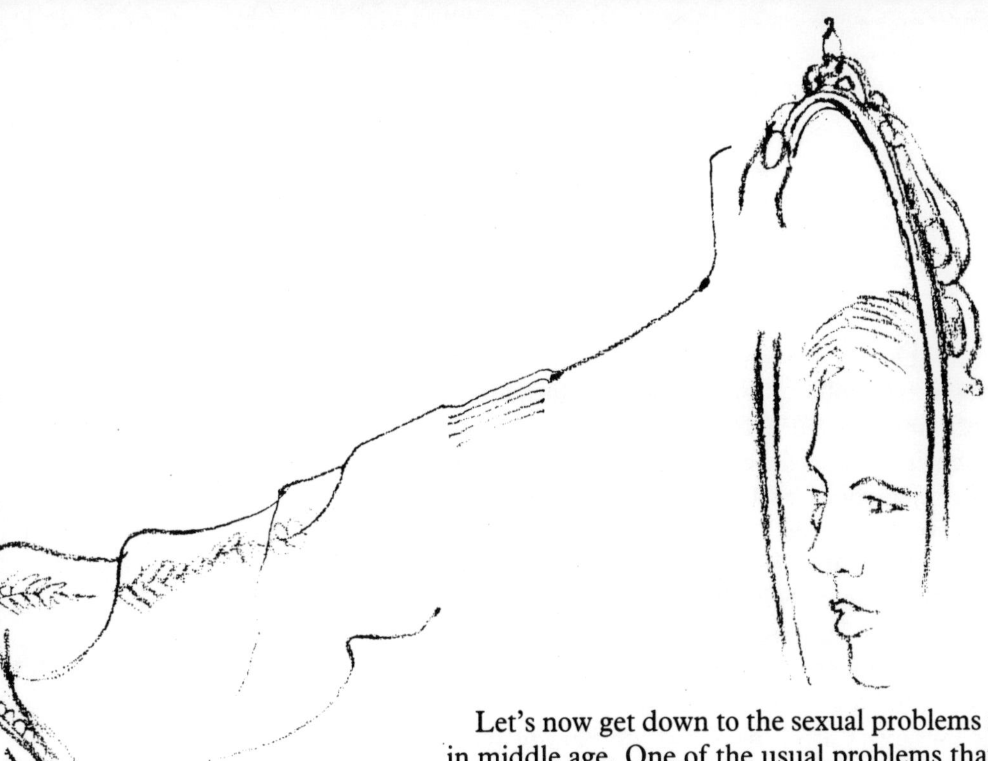

Let's now get down to the sexual problems most common amongst women in middle age. One of the usual problems that occurs after the menopause is that there may well be a lessening of vaginal lubrication and this may cause discomfort during intercourse. It's normally quite easy to overcome by using some lotion called KY Jelly from the chemist. If this doesn't do the trick, your doctor will be able to prescribe a hormone cream or even recommend some hormone replacement therapy (the latter is controversial due to possible side-effects and must be done in consultation with your doctor). When reading magazines like *Cosmopolitan* you'd think it was the main purpose in life, but this is nonsense of course and you don't have to have an orgasm to enjoy yourself. If you make love with the fixed idea that you must have an orgasm, you'll probably miss out on all the other sensual pleasures and end up disappointed, anxious and frustrated. Also, forget that you *have* to achieve orgasm together. That's another myth put out by sex books and novels; of course it's nice if it happens, but it's certainly not essential. Often the man can bring about a woman's orgasm completely separately by oral sex or clitorial stimulation. So stop trying to conform to what is 'normal' – concentrate on what pleases you most and forget any other ideas.

By the way, if you want to have a lot of love-making sessions and your partner is getting older, better results can be achieved if the man does not ejaculate every time. By saving it up you may find that you can both manage sex more frequently. One of the compensations of maturity is that a man will normally be able to hold his erection longer and have better control of ejaculation.

Sex on your own   Many of you reading this may be on your own with no husband, wife or lover and maybe feel a bit left out of it, so let's concentrate on you.

First, let me say firmly that sex is not essential for health and happiness and if for one reason or another you're not having sex, don't worry – nothing will drop off. Your mind and body will function perfectly well whether the abstinence is voluntary or forced; however, it's quite normal for some people without a partner to find physical relief in masturbation. Let's get rid of the awful myths and downright lies about it which have burdened so many people with guilt and shame for generations. I remember reading a Boy Scout book in my youth that called it 'self-abuse' and talked about draining one's manhood away – that scared me for years. Then there's the nonsense that it can cause ill health, acne and there's even a music hall joke that it can send you blind. In fact there's absolutely nothing wrong with masturbation, nearly all men and two-thirds of women have masturbated at some time. Lots of people do it as well as having sexual intercourse regularly. It's a pleasurable habit which doesn't harm anybody and is a convenient source of enjoyment. Both men and women use sexual fantasies and sometimes pornographic books as aids. The fantasies may be completely remote from anything they would do in reality, but who cares? Just don't feel guilty and depraved. A trip round a sex shop can be surprising, to say the least, with vibrators of every shape and size for ladies and even more exotic things for the men. For some women masturbation can even be a help to a better sex life with their partners, and sex therapists use it as a stage to help women who cannot usually reach orgasms with a partner.

Affairs Although adultery is one of the seven deadly sins it would be stupid not to admit that it goes on all the time.

Middle age is the period when there's probably the greatest danger of either partner becoming involved in love affairs. He, because he starts to get anxious about his looks and may perhaps be disappointed with his present sexual performance. She, for her part may be scared that her looks are beginning to fade and that she may not get many more romantic opportunities in the future. The main difference between them is that she's probably looking for romance rather than sex, and he's mainly interested in the sex side of it. Usually affairs are full of hazards. For those few blissful moments the couple became involved with so many lies, with 'best friends' involved to provide alibis. Split second timing becomes necessary, combined with frantic 'phone calls. There's usually plenty of discomfort too, if it's in the back of a car or a sordid little hotel room, and probably plenty of fear. It still goes on though – but why?

Perhaps it's for reassurance. It may be a terrific ego boost for the woman whilst going through the traumas of the menopause. For him, it may be the excitement of the chase with a new quarry. In a predictable, fairly dull, ordinary life it appears glamorous and daring. It's almost like thumbing your nose at respectable society for once. Another cause might be to escape possible tension and hostility within the marriage, or it may be simple loneliness when either partner is away for long periods of time, and then both may be tempted to have affairs. It doesn't necessarily mean that either party in a situation is wicked or deceitful, which is the usual label given by the injured party, but it's the injury to that third party of the triangle that can be so devastating as they go through the whole scale of emotions, all understandably distorted. For simplicity's sake let's call the other man or woman 'B'. At first, the husband or wife who has been 'wronged' may feel outraged at being deceived and humiliated and at being made to lose 'face', even worse when he or she is the last person to know about it. Your self-confidence and feelings of security go out of the window and you wonder what 'B's got that you haven't. The most self-destructive of all emotions is pure jealousy and that will probably come to the foremost. At this point

things must be put into perspective, which is often the hardest thing to do in such times of stress.

'Affairs' don't necessarily signify personal rejection or the end of a marriage. Obviously in the 'perfect' loving relationship you're never, ever tempted to stray from the fold, but not everyone is able to keep to this idyllic state for forty years or more. In France, because the Catholic faith forbids divorce, husbands, wives, lovers and mistresses all know exactly where they stand, and over the centuries a sort of compromise has developed. The French believe that the sensible way to treat infidelity is to turn a blind eye to it on the understanding that they miss out as little as possible on everything else in marriage. This kind of 'open relationship' may suit a lot of couples but it's important to discuss it and both be agreed that it's what *both* partners want in order to avoid any hurt and confusion in the future. The intensity and the duration of these feelings may depend on whether it's a serious threat to the marriage or a relatively minor indiscretion. Of course, the person who is having the affair may be a compulsive philanderer whose compulsiveness can be almost likened to that of an alcoholic, combined with a very real terror of losing a spouse.

My own wife has had experience of almost every marital permutation during her thirteen years as a marriage guidance counsellor. Counsellors, in spite of their unjustified 'do-gooding', middle-class image are well-trained, sympathetic and unshockable. They provide an excellent sounding board for emotional troubles, and although they won't give any actual advice they do offer an unbiased third party, making communication between two perhaps hostile people very much easier. Appointments, either singly or together can be made by telephone, and you will find the number in your local 'phone directory. However, the final result will depend on how strongly the couple is committed to each other, and their limits of tolerance and love, together with the belief each has in the lasting worth of their marriage.

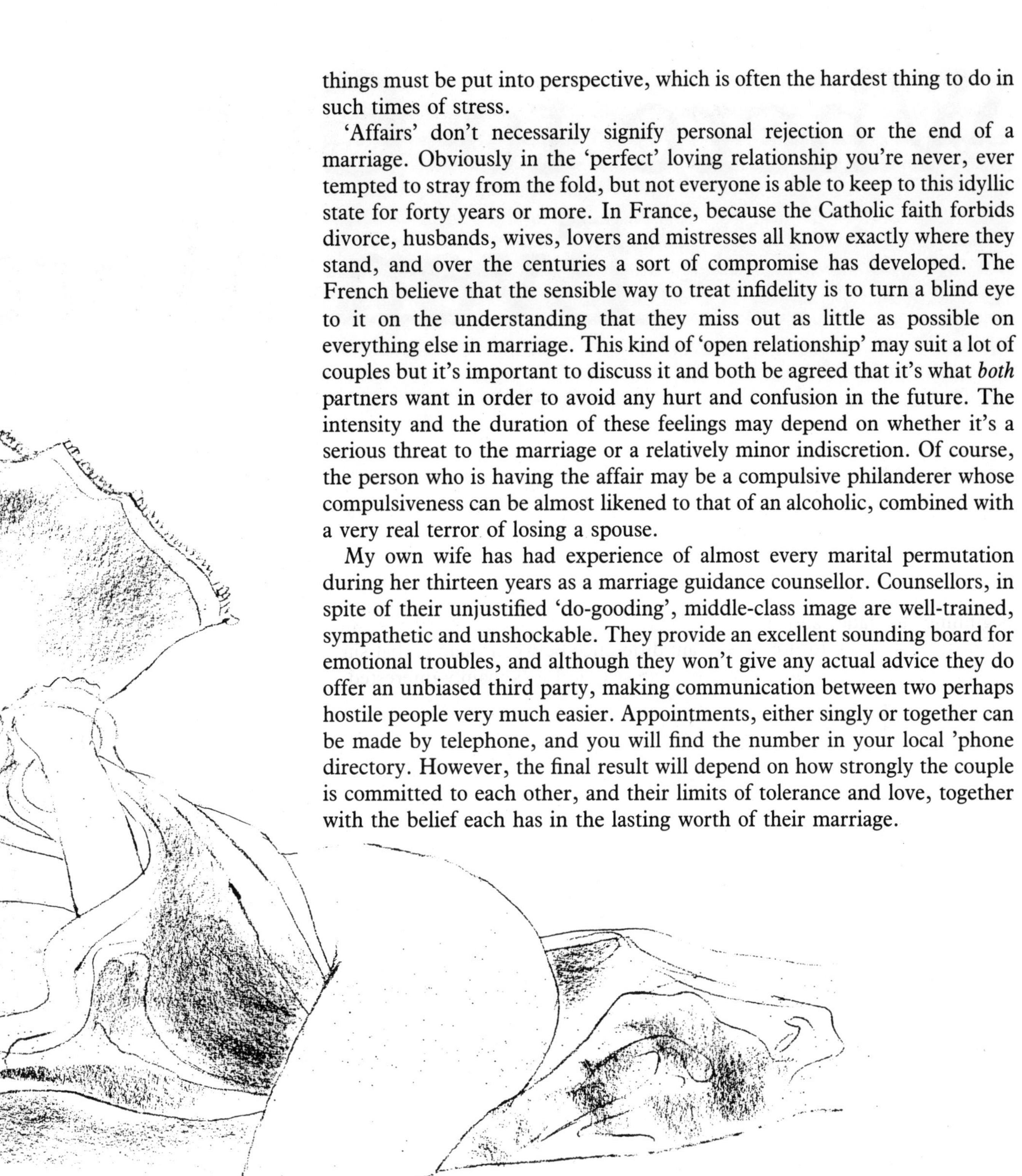

Chapter 15

Where to Get Even More

Help

This chapter is a list of books and addresses which you will find useful. They cover all areas mentioned in previous chapters, and I have no hesitation at all in recommending them as they're all tried, tested and readily available.

Taking action   Christie & Co and Wessex Sales Organisation are two examples of the type of agent described that deal with small retail businesses. Wessex Sales are at Wessex House, 23 Halsbury Road, Westbury Park, Bristol BS6 7SS, and Christie & Co are based at 32 Baker Street, London W1M 2BU. Christie & Co has also published books on this subject which can be obtained from the Book Sales Department, 1 Walter's Yard, High Street, Bromley, Kent.

British Franchise Association, which will supply a Franchisee Information Pack, is to be found at Franchise Chambers, 75a Bell Street, Henley-on-Thames, Oxon RG9 2BD (0491-578049).

Promoting yourself   Mentioned in this chapter is the Registry of Business Names and you'll find these at the following addresses: For England and Wales, The Registrar of Business Names, Pembroke House, 40-56 City Road, London EC1 2DN (01-253-9393); for Scotland, The Registrar of Business Names, 102 George Street, Edinburgh EH2 3DJ (031-225-5774/5) and for Northern Ireland, The Department of Commerce, Registry of Business Names, 43-47 Chichester Street, Belfast BT1 4RJ (Belfast 34121/4).

Calling in the experts   You can find the whereabout and 'phone number of the Department of Industry's Small Firms Service Division by 'phoning the operator at your local exchange and asking for Freefone 2444 or by writing to Abell House, John Islip Street, London SW1P 4LN (01-211-3040).

The address of the Council for Small Industries in Rural Areas (CoSIRA) is Queens House, 141 Castle Street, Salisbury, Wilts SP1 3TP. The Welsh Development Agency, Small Business Unit is at Treforest Industrial Estate, Pontypridd, Mid-Glamorgan CF37 5CT, and the Scottish Development Agency, Small Business Section at 102 Telford Road, Edinburgh EH4 2NP.

URBED, 359 Strand, London WC2R 0HP and the London Enterprise Agency at the London Chamber of Commerce and Industry, 69 Cannon Street, London EC4N 5AB will also be pleased to help.

If you're stuck as to which accountant to go to, you might like to contact the Association of Certified Accountants, 22 Bedford Square, London WC1B 3HS (01-636-2103).

Another good idea is to join the National Federation of Self-Employed and Small Businesses at 32 St Annes Road West, Lytham St Annes, Lancs. It has over 50,000 members, including fifty MPs, in 370 branches throughout the UK and operates a free legal protection scheme for members. Their aim is to protect small businesses from more legislation and what they call 'bureaucratic suffocation'.

Money matters   As well as the books and associations already mentioned which you'll find useful on this subject, there is a book by Richard Edwards called *Running your own Business*, which also gives advice on how to keep your books.

The ICFC (Industrial & Commercial Finance Corporation) are at 91 Waterloo Road, London SE1 8XP and the Department of Trade's Small Firms Division will also provide helpful information.

Taxes and how to lesson them   A fairly easy-to-read book on this rather daunting subject has been written by Richard Edwards, *Tax for the Self-Employed* (published by Oyez Longman).

Insuring yourself   You'll find some interesting additional reading on this subject in the Consumers' Association – *Starting Your Own Business* from the publishers of *Which?* In particular, it has a very good chapter covering all kinds of insurance.

Coping with the law   Most of the books mentioned will provide at least some extra information on this subject, but two leaflets dealing with specifics are *Letting Rooms in Your Home* (published by the Department of the Environment), and *Your Guide to the Food Hygiene (General) Regulations 1970* (published by the Health Education Council at 78 New Oxford Street, London WC1A 1AH.

Health   There are three books which between them tell you all you need to know about your general health and give lots of straightforward information and advice, they are as follows: *The Sunday Times New Book of Body*

Maintenance (published by Peerage Books); *The BUPA Manual of Fitness and Well Being* (published by Macdonald); *Readers' Digest Family Medical Adviser*.

An excellent and fairly new service is run by the College of Health, 18 Victoria Park Square, London, E2 9PF, called Healthline. You can dial 01-980-4848 between 6pm and 9pm, and ask to listen to tapes on a whole range of health topics. By the time you read this, there may well be a Healthline near you. The only cost is that of the 'phone call.

More specifically, there are books and associations dealing with diseases of middle age, smoking, and alcoholism which may also be very useful. For diseases in middle age, as well as the books mentioned above, there is a booklet called *Avoiding Heart Attacks*, which is part of DHSS Prevention and Health and is obtainable from HMSO (addresses in your 'phone book). Another is a *Which?* book called *Living Through Middle Age*.

A group called The Coronary Prevention Group, Central Middlesex Hospital, London, NW10 7NS, will give lots of advice and support if necessary, and the Health Education Council at 78 New Oxford Street, London WC1, print some very useful leaflets, especially *Looking After Yourself*.

Additional reading about the effects of smoking includes a very good chapter in *The Book of Body Maintenance* – 'Smoking or Health?', which is a report by the Royal College of Physicians and again the *Which?* book *Living Through Middle Age*. A useful society to know about is Action on Smoking and Health, ASH, Margaret Pyke House, 27-35 Mortimer Street, London W1. The books which deal with smoking also offer good advice on alcoholism and very clear information is provided in the *Reader's Digest Family Medical Adviser*. There are several addresses to contact for advice and support, probably the best known one is AA (Alcoholics Anonymous), 11 Redcliffe Gardens, London SW10 9BG, 01-834-8202 for London, or 01-352-9779 for the rest of the country. Others are ACCEPT, Western Hospital, Seagrave Road, London SWG 1R2 (01-381-3155), and Alcohol Concern, 3 Grosvenor Crescent SW1X 7EE (01-235-4182). In Scotland, Scottish Council on Alcoholism, 147 Blythswood Street, Glasgow G24EN (041-333-9677) and in Northern Ireland, Northern Ireland Council on Alcohol, 40 Elmwood Avenue, Belfast, B79 6AZ (0232-664434). A group which helps family units is Al-Anon Family Groups, U.K. and Eire, 61 Great Dover Street SE1 4YF (01-403-0888).

Turning to keep-fit and slimming, there are many clubs and associations spread all over the country, including what seem to be the three major slimming clubs: Weight Watchers, Slimming Magazine and Silhouette. These are advertised widely and you'll probably be able to find one near you. Many local authorities run various types of keep-fit classes or you may be near enough to make use of one of their swimming pools. Two additional books which you may find useful on this subject are *Which? Way to Slim* and *The Sunday Times ABC Diet and Body Plan* (published by Hutchinson).

General reading – there are many other books in the shops and libraries dealing with the subject of this book, but here are four which will more than repay you for the time you may spend reading them. *How to Earn a Second Income* by Godfrey Golzen (published by Frederick Muller) has much in it which is in fact relevant to a sole income as much as a second. *Small Businesses – How They Survive and Succeed* by Philip Clarke (published by David & Charles) details the actual experiences of many small businesses. *How to be your Own Boss* by Conrad Frost (published by Macmillan's Paperbacks). Last but quite definitely not least is a book written especially for women on their own, *On Your Own* by Jean Shapiro (published by Pandora Books).

Index